CONTENTS

Chapter One: Bereavement Issues

Chapter Two: Grief and Young People

Chapter Three: Handling the Formalities

Introduction

Grief and Loss is the one hundred and sixteenth volume in the ***Issues*** series. The aim of this series is to offer up-to-date information about important issues in our world.

Grief and Loss looks at the issues raised by a bereavement, the problems of young people and children who have been bereaved, and dealing with the formalities of a bereavement such as funeral arrangements.

The information comes from a wide variety of sources and includes:
Government reports and statistics
Newspaper reports and features
Magazine articles and surveys
Website material
Literature from lobby groups
and charitable organisations.

It is hoped that, as you read about the many aspects of the issues explored in this book, you will critically evaluate the information presented. It is important that you decide whether you are being presented with facts or opinions. Does the writer give a biased or an unbiased report? If an opinion is being expressed, do you agree with the writer?

Grief and Loss offers a useful starting-point for those who need convenient access to information about the many issues involved. However, it is only a starting-point. Following each article is a URL to the relevant organisation's website, which you may wish to visit for further information.

*****

Bereavement

Information from BUPA

Bereavement means, literally, to be deprived by death. After someone close to you dies, you go through a process of mourning. Numbness, anger and sadness can all be part of that process. Bereavement can also cause physical reactions including sleeplessness, loss of energy and loss of appetite.

Grief is normal

When someone is bereaved, they usually experience an intense feeling of sorrow – grief. People grieve in order to accept a deep loss and carry on with their life. Experts believe that if you do not grieve at the time of death, or shortly after, the grief may stay bottled up inside you. This can cause emotional problems or physical illness later on. Working through your grief can be a painful process, but it is often necessary to ensure your future emotional and physical well-being.

The stages of grief

There is no single way to grieve. Everyone is different and each person grieves in his or her own way. However, some stages of grief are commonly experienced by people when they are bereaved. There is no set timescale for these stages to be reached, but it can be helpful to be aware of the stages and to consider that intense emotions and swift changes in mood are normal.

Feeling emotionally numb is often the first reaction to a loss, and may last for a few hours, days or longer. In some ways, this numbness can help you get through the practical arrangements and family pressures that surround the funeral, but if this phase goes on for too long, it could be a problem.

The numbness may be replaced by a deep yearning for the person who has died. You may feel agitated or angry, and find it difficult to concentrate, relax or sleep. You may also feel guilty, dwelling on arguments you had with that person or on emotions and words you wished you had expressed.

This period of strong emotion usually gives way to bouts of intense sadness, silence and withdrawal from family and friends. During this time, you may be prone to sudden outbursts of tears, set off by reminders and memories of the dead person.

Over time, the pain, sadness and depression starts to lessen. You begin to see your life in a more positive light again, although it is important to acknowledge that you may not completely overcome the feeling of loss.

The final phase of grieving is to let go of the person who has died and move on with your life. This helps sadness to clear, and your sleeping patterns and energy levels to return to normal.

Children and bereavement

Children are aware when a loved one dies and they feel that loss in much the same way as adults do. Children go through similar stages of grief, although they may progress through them more quickly. Understandably, some people try to protect children from the death and grieving process. But in fact, it is better to be honest with children about your own grief, and encourage them to talk about feelings of pain and distress in their turn.

How long does grieving take?

The grieving process can take time and should not be hurried. How long it takes depends on you and your situation. In general, though, it takes most people one to two years to recover from a major bereavement.

Coping with the grief process

There are many things you can do to help yourself cope during this time. Ask for help and support from family, friends or a support group. Try to express whatever you are feeling, be

Some people may find it impossible to acknowledge the bereavement at all, which can mean that their feelings are not worked through properly

it anger, guilt or sadness. Accept that some things, like death, are beyond your control. Avoid making major decisions – your judgement may be off kilter and changes could increase your stress levels. Give yourself the time and space to grieve. By doing so, you are able to mourn properly and avoid problems in the future.

What if you aren't coping?

Sometimes, the grieving process is especially difficult. Some people may find it impossible to acknowledge the bereavement at all, which can mean that their feelings are not worked through properly. Others may be unable to move on from their grief, making it impossible to rebuild their lives. Certain factors can make a difficult bereavement more likely:

■ being male
■ several previous bereavements
■ a history of mental illness, such as depression, anxiety or previous suicide attempts
■ a dependent relationship with

the person who has died, or a relationship where you had troubled or negative feelings about the deceased

■ low self-esteem
■ a lack of support from family and friends.

Bereavement can also cause particular problems for the bereaved in certain circumstances around the death. These can include:

■ a sudden or unexpected death
■ the death of a parent when you are a child or adolescent
■ miscarriage or the death of a baby
■ death due to AIDS or suicide
■ the death of a co-habiting partner, same-sex partner or partner from an extra-marital relationship, where the relationship may not be legally recognised or accepted by family and friends
■ a death involving murder, legal proceedings or media coverage
■ deaths where the bereaved may be responsible
■ situations where a post mortem or an inquest is required
■ more than one death at once (for example, in an accident).

Getting help from your GP

There are many ways your GP can help. For instance, if you are sleeping badly, they may be able to prescribe you a few days' supply of sleeping tablets, such as loprazolam. These

Helping family or friends

If somebody in your family or a friend has been bereaved, the best thing you can do is spend time with them, and listen to them work through their grief. Offer practical help, such as cooking dinner or shopping for food – when a person is grieving, it is usually hard to focus on everyday tasks. Finally, if the person is reacting in extreme ways for a prolonged period, encourage him or her to seek professional help.

should only be used in the short-term.

If your feelings of depression are worsening, affecting your energy, appetite and sleep, your GP may prescribe antidepressants. If things don't get better, your GP may also refer you to see a specialist, perhaps a psychiatrist. For more information, please see the separate BUPA factsheets, *Depression* and *Depression treatments*.

There are also other useful talking therapies that can help. These include bereavement counselling and psychotherapy, as well as support groups where you can meet with other people who have been bereaved.

Further information

Cruse Bereavement Care
0870 167 1677
http://www.crusebereavementcare.org.uk

The Royal College of Psychiatrists
020 7235 2351
http://www.rcpsych.ac.uk

National Association of Bereavement Services
020 7709 0505
020 7709 9090 (helpline)
Open 10.00 am to 4.00 pm weekdays; messages can be left at any time.

■ The above information is reprinted with kind permission from BUPA, excluding any accopanying illustrations, diagrams and graphs. Visit www.bupa.co.uk/health for more information.

© BUPA

Experience of bereavement

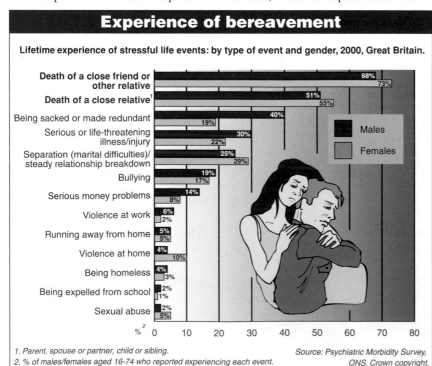

Lifetime experience of stressful life events: by type of event and gender, 2000, Great Britain.

Event	Males	Females
Death of a close friend or other relative	68%	73%
Death of a close relative[1]	51%	55%
Being sacked or made redundant	40%	19%
Serious or life-threatening illness/injury	30%	22%
Separation (marital difficulties)/ steady relationship breakdown	25%	29%
Bullying	19%	17%
Serious money problems	14%	8%
Violence at work	6%	2%
Running away from home	5%	5%
Violence at home	4%	10%
Being homeless	4%	3%
Being expelled from school	2%	1%
Sexual abuse	2%	5%

%[2] 0 10 20 30 40 50 60 70 80

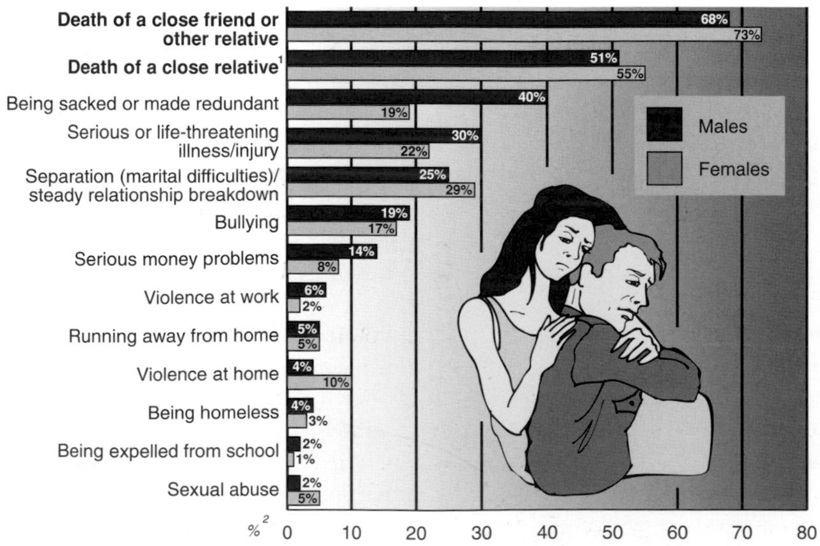

1. Parent, spouse or partner, child or sibling.
2. % of males/females aged 16-74 who reported experiencing each event.

Source: Psychiatric Morbidity Survey, ONS. Crown copyright.

Understanding bereavement

Information from Mind

'Why did it have to happen? Why do I have to go through this? Why did he have to leave me?'
'I feel like I'm going on automatic pilot.'
'If only I'd done more, maybe he would still have been alive.'
'If I could just have talked to somebody else, just to somebody else that it had happened to.'

This article helps those who are facing the loss of someone close to them to know better what to expect from themselves and others. It provides information for them, their families and friends about how to cope, and what support is available.

Why do we need to grieve?

The death of someone we love is emotionally devastating. It may be the greatest loss that we will ever have to contend with. Yet death is an unavoidable part of life, however little we like it.

One in four adults will have experienced the death of someone close to them within the past five years. For some people, this will be one of many experiences of bereavement; for others it

For better
mental health

will be their first encounter with death. Its impact can vary from the bearably painful to the emotionally catastrophic.

Mourning is the way we come to terms with bereavement. It's about letting go of the person we have lost; gradually changing the nature of the bonds that attached us to them. We have to come to accept that we will never see that person again in this life. If we try to avoid this natural process, we will be unable to live fully for the rest of our lives, and could be storing up trouble for ourselves later on.

The funeral, marking the end of the first few days, is an important part of the grieving process. Funerals offer the best chance to remember the life of the person who has died, to say goodbye to them and to share that farewell with other mourners. In acknowledging death we affirm life.

In marking the passing of the one we have loved, in the company of friends and family, we also affirm the values of our community and strengthen the bonds between those left alive. These bonds are necessary to life and to the process of mourning.

The funeral is very important, but it is only the first part of the grieving process. Grieving is not much understood or acknowledged in our society. We are supposed to be happy consumers, and are discouraged from 'being morbid'. Death and grieving have become as taboo to us as sex was to the Victorians. Yet acknowledging the emotions surrounding death is just as important to our emotional wellbeing.

Why do people react differently?

There are no rules about the natural process of grieving, it's a different experience for everyone and reactions will vary. They will usually depend on your previous relationship with the dead person and how you felt about them, as well as on your own personal history.

The circumstances of the death will also affect your grief. The death of an older person who has lived a long and full life will feel appropriate, no matter how saddening. But the death of your child, or a miscarriage, can seem unbearable and may never make sense to you; it may be hard not to feel that this is a 'wasted life'. For a survivor of someone who has committed suicide, it's a question of facing a death that is, more often than not, unexpected, untimely and possibly violent.

How might people respond?

People experience a variety of possible physical and emotional responses to losing someone. You may feel depressed, permanently exhausted or full of aches and pains. You will probably expect to feel sad, but, instead, you may feel numb to begin with, void of any feeling. Your typical response to everything may be slow, automatic and cold. This is to do with being in shock.

Shock is usually associated with sudden death, but even when a death has long been expected, you may still experience shock when you hear the news. There are many practical arrangements to be made after someone dies. You may find yourself carrying out these tasks in a perfectly competent way, while feeling quite divorced from what is going on around you. You may even find it hard to cry. Because you are not 'breaking down' other people may assume that you are uncaring or stoical. Or they may tell you that you are coping well. Take no notice of such opinions. The shock may be a useful protection, which gets you through the first few days.

Some people may find it difficult to concentrate, to sort out priorities or even to order their thoughts. Tasks that are usually relatively simple to perform may become major obstacles or feel too difficult to handle. You may find yourself unable to cope with all the arrangements you need to make. Do allow willing helpers to support you through this.

A feeling of disbelief is a common and, usually, passing reaction to a bereavement. It may be more likely among people who didn't get a chance to say goodbye, because they weren't there or didn't see the body afterwards. If the death was sudden (because of a heart attack or a road traffic accident, for instance), it can, naturally, take longer to accept its reality.

Apart from feeling very weepy, people often become apathetic, withdrawn or very tired. They may have problems sleeping and lose their appetite. Although these physical effects and sensations may be frightening, they are not, in themselves, any cause for concern, provided that they don't go on for too long.

It's perfectly natural to feel relief, too, because someone's suffering is over, or because a long period of uncertainty has come to an end. It's also quite common to feel anxious.

You may fear you'll be overwhelmed by grief or that you can't survive without the person you loved. You may become more aware of danger and of death, in general, and develop a much stronger sense of your own mortality. This can leave you feeling very insecure. Some people suffer from panic attacks, experiencing a rapid build-up of overpowering sensations, such as a pounding heart, faintness or shaky limbs, which make them fear that they are going mad, will black out or are having a heart attack.

You may find that you feel very guilty, accusing yourself of all sorts of things. Sometimes people get stuck with regrets about things left undone – a sense of 'if only'. On the other hand, you may feel guilty because the death, following a long illness, has now relieved you of a burden that was hard to cope with. There is usually no need to feel guilty.

Grief often gives rise to anger. The bereaved person may feel very angry at the person who has died for leaving them and causing them such pain. They may feel unable to admit this to themselves, and instead become bitterly angry with someone else, for instance the health system, a family member, the Government or God. This is why it's so common for family feuds to start at funerals! We are encouraged to idealise the dead; it can be hard to admit how angry we are with them.

It's important to recognise that we are justified in feeling angry about neglectful doctors, careless drivers, or with anyone whose actions really contributed to the death. But we also need to acknowledge, sometimes, that the dead person was not perfect. We may have many reasons for being angry with them for things they did or didn't do in life. We also need to recognise that we can be angry with them just for dying, for leaving us to face life without them. It's not a comfortable feeling, and not rational. But it's a normal reaction.

After the funeral, people often realise how lonely they feel. That special person who made life meaningful and pleasurable, who made them feel good, has suddenly gone, and everything can feel hopeless and futile.

A lack of family or other social support for the relationship can make the mourning process even more difficult. You may have been a partner in a gay or lesbian relationship, which family and friends may not have known about. You may be feeling even more isolated because your loss can't be openly acknowledged. It's especially important not to remain isolated, but to forge links with friends or networks that will support you and value your relationship with the deceased.

This distressing and difficult period sometimes breeds suicidal thoughts. There are a number of support groups that can provide invaluable help at such times. But it's important to remember that relatively few people actually commit suicide following the loss of someone they loved.

How long does mourning take?

Grieving is a process that can take a long time. A bereaved person needs support from friends and family. It can also help if they have a strong spiritual belief system and regular spiritual practice. Over time, grief will resolve itself, although this can take a year or two.

Depression is a condition with symptoms very similar to those of grieving

There are some factors that can make grief likely to be more prolonged. This can happen, for example, in the following circumstances:

- The grieving person is socially isolated, has no community or social support, and no spiritual practice or belief system.
- The mourner had unfinished business with the dead person, such as old quarrels which were never made up, or love or anger that were never spoken enough.
- The circumstances of the death were difficult. For example, if the death was part of a controversial disaster, such as the Madrid train bombings or the events at Hillsborough football stadium.

Or if the people responsible are never brought to justice, or the trial is flawed, as in the Stephen Lawrence case.

- The person is missing, and there is no definite news of their fate. This often happens during a war or disasters such as the tsunami in South East Asia and the destruction of the World Trade Centre in New York.
- There was no funeral, or the mourner could not go. This may be because they were on the other side of the world at the time, because no one told them about it, or because their relation to the dead person was not socially acknowledged. (For example, they may have been lovers, but the dead person was married to someone else.)

All these can make the grieving process more difficult, and may mean that it takes longer.

Mourning and depression

Depression is a condition with symptoms very similar to those of grieving, such as appetite loss or overeating, not sleeping properly, suicidal thoughts, not being able to concentrate, feeling tearful or numb, losing interest in sex, and generally being in a low mood. But while grief is a process that people move through, depression has a stuck quality to it. It goes on and on and does not change. Grief can usually be linked to a particular event involving loss; depression may come on at any time, apparently out of the blue. Or it may set in during the grieving process, if the person gets stuck in grief and can't move on.

One cause of depression can be that the person has unresolved grief from a past loss, which they have not mourned fully. This is particularly true of losses in childhood. Such losses could have been obviously traumatic ones, such as the serious illness or death of a parent, which adults would recognise. There may also have been events, such as moving house, emigrating, or the death of a pet, which can be much harder for a child to deal with than for an adult. What is important is not so much the degree of loss, but the way in which it was dealt with by those caring for the child. Children are very resilient and can survive amazing stress and losses with the right kind of support. But if a person had to cope alone, unable to talk about what has happened or to grieve over it, even an apparently trivial loss, such as moving house, can have serious long-term consequences for their mental health.

Coming to terms with your loss is a gradual process and, like all healing, it takes time. Be patient with yourself

In such a case, an event in adult life, such as the death of someone close, the retirement of a colleague or other events involving loss, can bring on depression. It reminds them, unconsciously, of the unfinished business of mourning. It's very important, if this happens, that the person finds someone to talk to, so that they can finish their mourning and find a fuller and more joyous life in the present. (See Mind's booklets *Understanding depression* and *Understanding talking treatments*.)

What's the best way for me to cope?

Looking after yourself when you are grieving may not be easy, or foremost in your mind. Acknowledging your feelings and expressing them is a vital part of the natural, healing process, however. Grieving is hard work; exhausting and stressful. You need to look after yourself; body, mind and spirit. Physically, your immune system is likely to be depleted. You need good food (especially fresh fruit and vegetables, or failing that, a Vitamin C supplement), plenty of rest, and the right amount of exercise.

Emotionally, you need to express your grief. Do whatever feels right for you. If you want to spend time poring over old photos and crying over a favourite jumper that reminds you of a special time together, then do so! The arts, especially music (either listening to it, singing or playing it yourself) can be very helpful at this time. Talking with others who share your grief is very important. You might also want to make pilgrimages to places you associate with the lost person, to paint pictures of your grief or write stories or poems. The important thing is to keep it flowing.

This can be very difficult in a culture that does not support the grieving process. You may well come under pressure from colleagues or family to be brave or snap out of it. This is not helpful advice. What you need is time and space to express your grief, so avoid those who want to deny it to you, if you can.

How long will I go on feeling this way?

Coming to terms with your loss is a gradual process and, like all healing, it takes time. Be patient with yourself. You will almost certainly find that there is no single cut-off point when your grieving stops. There are likely to be days when you feel you may have achieved it, and others when you reach the depths of despair again.

At some point, you will realise that thoughts of the dead person aren't constantly filling your mind, and when you do remember them, it's not always with sadness. You may notice, for example, that you are just beginning to make plans for the future. Don't feel guilty about that; love doesn't have to be measured by sorrow. For some people, the timing of this turning point coincides with a particular anniversary. A first anniversary of the death is often a watershed, but other yearly celebrations and special occasions, such as birthdays or wedding days, may re-awaken some sadness. This will probably lessen each year.

As time goes by, you may realise that you are dwelling less on the past. You will find yourself looking ahead, planning and starting new projects. This is perfectly natural; although life can't go on exactly as before, you do have a future.

■ The above information is reprinted with kind permission from Mind. Please visit their website at www.mind.org.uk for more information.

Grief counselling a waste of time, say psychologists

By Raj Persaud

Bereavement counselling – long considered by psychologists to be vital in recovering from the death of a loved one – may be a waste of time, according to a new study.

The research challenges a belief that has been firmly held by psychoanalysts since Sigmund Freud proposed in 1917 that confronting feelings is the healthiest way to cope with bereavement.

Many psychoanalysts have even argued that failure to express grief indicates – or may lead to – deep psychological problems.

Sigmund Freud proposed in 1917 that confronting feelings is the healthiest way to cope with bereavement

These days, bereavement counsellors often urge people to express their sadness in order to release 'suppressed emotions'. Now, however, a group of psychologists from Utrecht University in the Netherlands, who carried out their own research and reviewed that of others, has found no link between emotional expression of grief and a lessening of subsequent distress.

They assessed 128 recently bereaved people four times over two years and found no significant statistical difference between the continued distress in those who shared their emotions and those who did not.

The authors, Wolfgang Stroebe, Henk Schut and Margaret Stroebe, whose research is published this week in the *Clinical Psychology Review*, also challenged the view that it is beneficial for those who have suffered loss to 'write about their very deepest thoughts and feelings'.

They reviewed previous trials in which bereaved people had been asked to write for 15 to 30 minutes either about a recent traumatic loss or a trivial topic, and found little evidence that writing about emotions was beneficial.

The authors said: 'The findings challenge beliefs about grief work, emotional disclosure and beneficial interventions that were considered as self-evident by bereavement researchers only a decade ago.'

They claimed that counselling was more likely to benefit those with 'complicated' grief – such as those whose loved ones suffered a particularly traumatic death.

Why, the researchers then asked, do bereaved people with

'uncomplicated' grief fail to benefit from 'grief work'?

They concluded that the most common difficulty suffered by bereaved people is emotional loneliness: the feeling of being utterly alone, even when in the company of friends and family. This type of loneliness, they say, only abates with time and nothing can be done to aid recovery.

The findings are supported by Dr Colin Murray Parkes, a consultant psychiatrist and the president of the charity Cruse Bereavement Care.

He said: 'There is no evidence that all bereaved people will benefit from counselling, and research has shown no benefit to arise from the routine referral of people to counselling for no other reason than that they have suffered bereavement.'

■ Dr Raj Persaud is the Gresham Professor for Public Understanding of Psychiatry

Feelings on bereavement

Information from Supportline

When you lose someone close to you at times the emotional pain can be so intense and overwhelming that you think that feeling will never end; you cannot see how you could ever be happy again or continue with life. The hurt and pain can seem so personal – this is something which has happened to you and nobody else – but it does help to keep reminding yourself that however hard and painful it is to bear the loss of a loved one, it is nevertheless part of life; it will happen to everyone at some stage or another.

Anyone who has been bereaved will know that your feelings can change very quickly from one minute to the next. One minute you may feel you are coping and the next you are dragged back into the depths of despair, feeling there is no point in going on. The reality is that grief does run its course; although it does not feel like it, time is a healer, and if you allow yourself to grieve you should get to a stage where you can remember the person who has died and focus on the good memories. You can still miss the person terribly, but it won't be affecting your everyday life or stopping you from moving on with your own life. When you get to that stage, yes there will be sadness when you remember your loved one but the enormous feeling of pain will have faded.

You may feel angry at the person who has died for leaving you on your own, or you may feel guilty at having wished the person would die, for instance in cases of a severely ill person who was suffering pain and a poor quality of life – these are perfectly normal feelings to have; try and express how you feel rather than keeping those feelings inside you.

Everyone's reaction to grief is different but it is healthy and natural to express emotion – to get out your pain, anger, hurt, frustration, loneliness – rather than suppressing feelings which can ultimately make

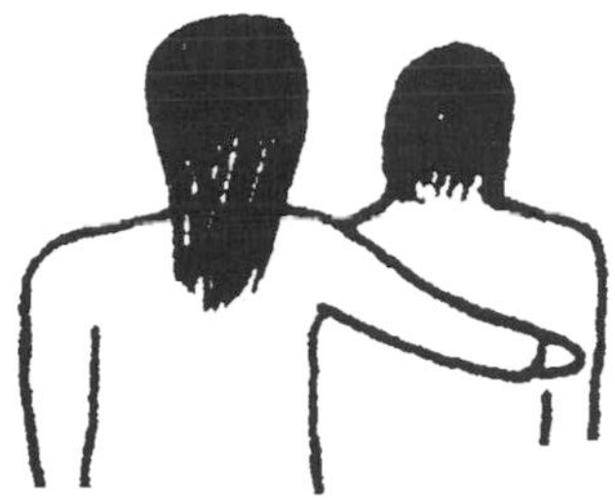

it harder to go through the grieving process and move on. You may find that family, friends, etc. do not allow you to talk about the person who has died, or they may avoid talking about the person who has died, or they may tell you not to cry – people are often afraid to talk because they feel it would cause you more distress to mention the person. However many people who are bereaved want to talk and want to cry and this should be encouraged – if you are in a situation where you do not have people in your life to talk to there are helplines and counsellors who will allow you to talk and help you to grieve.

Don't be afraid to say to people that it helps you to talk and you want to talk. Sometimes other people just don't know the best way to help you or what they can say to help – when someone is grieving words can seem so meaningless and empty and other people cannot guess what will help you in your grief.

It is common for some people to feel 'disloyal' to the person who has died by 'feeling better' – however, the reality is that by 'feeling better' it does not mean the person means any less to you, just that you have accepted the reality that the person has gone. In order to carry on living you need to be able to let go of the person who has died, and if you are finding that difficult and a considerable period of time has elapsed since the person died, you may find that counselling will help you to let go. Holding on to pain will not help you to keep hold of the person you have lost, and ultimately the person who has died would want you to move on with your life. If it helps to talk to the person who has died, to look at photos, to go to places where they enjoyed going, that is a way of keeping their memory alive; but try not to stop it from allowing you to meet other people, to get on with your everyday living, to do things you enjoy, etc.

One of the difficult things to come to terms with – particularly with a sudden death – is that you may not have had time to say goodbye and all the things you wanted to say. To move on you need to allow yourself to say these things. Some people find it helps to go to a quiet place – maybe somewhere you know the person who has died would have liked – and to speak out loud as if the person was there, about everything you would have liked to have said before the person died, or some people find it helps to write a letter to the person

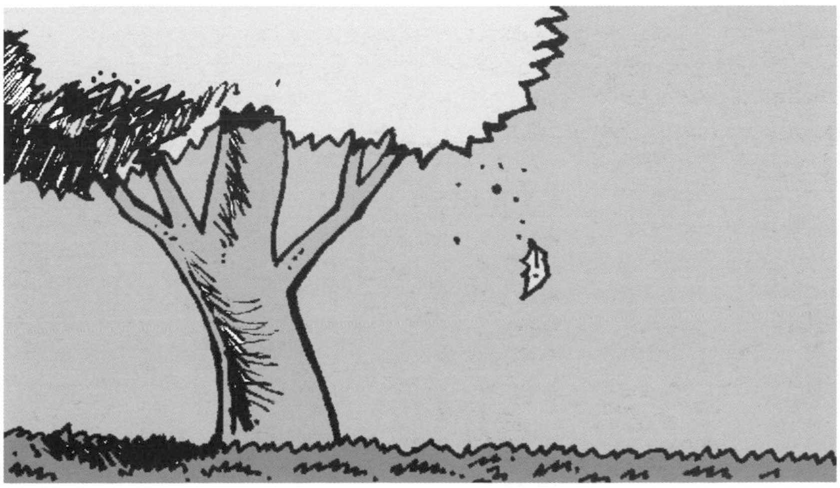

who died and include in it everything they wanted to say. Find whatever way suits you, and which enables you to say everything you would have liked to have said but didn't.

Bereaved by murder

In some ways we can make sense of death when we have lost someone through an illness and we may be able to rationalise and accept that this is part of life. In deaths where a loved one may have been murdered, or may have been killed in a car accident by a speeding dangerous driver, it can be impossible to rationalise and make sense of because it is not a 'normal' part of life so you can't comfort yourself with that knowledge. It is natural to have enormous feelings of anger, rage, hatred, and wanting to take revenge against the person who has taken away your loved one. There is no way you can make sense of the unjustness of it and you have to get your feelings out in a safe way.

In some ways we can make sense of death when we have lost someone through an illness

However hard it may be, you have to try and find a way of reconciling yourself to what has happened, however unfair, unjust or wrong, it is, as the alternative is that if you allow your life to be consumed with hatred, bitterness and rage it will in effect destroy your life and possibly the lives of those closest to you. This will mean the person or persons responsible for taking away your loved one will have destroyed not only their life but your life and others as well. Some people find that in situations like this it helps them to be able to talk to others who have been through a similar situation and there are agencies specifically for helping people who have had someone close to them murdered, killed in a road accident etc.

Some people find it helps to turn their anger into a positive force by becoming involved in a support group and working perhaps for more help for victims of crime, proper and just sentencing for offenders etc. Do whatever is going to help you to move on with your life, to help you to find some meaning in life again, to be able to enjoy things in life, to be able to laugh and look forward to things, because that is what your loved one would want – they would not want your life to be destroyed as well.

Bereaved by suicide

If you have lost someone through suicide the pain is unbearable and the constant question of 'why' goes round and round in your head.

It is common for anyone bereaved by suicide to blame themselves – maybe I should have given the person more time, maybe I didn't listen enough, I should have picked up on the warning signs, I had a big row with him/her before he/she committed suicide, if only I had come back home earlier, if only I hadn't gone out, if only, if only, if only.

There is also so much anger – how can he/she have done that and left me? There are people who think that suicide is a cowardly thing to do and an easy way out. However, if you were able to understand the intensity of the pain that the suicidal person feels and the immense struggle they have over what they are going to do, in no way is it an easy way out.

A person who is suicidal is so overwhelmed with feelings of despair and hopelessness that the intensity of their feelings takes over everything else. At that moment in time they honestly feel that their loved ones would be better off without them, they may feel that they are a burden or that their problems are a burden to those around them and may not be able to think rationally about what their loss would really mean to others.

You cannot live your life thinking what if I had done this or that, because at the end of the day if a person is determined to commit suicide it doesn't matter how much support and help they are given – they may still think that the pain and hurt they are feeling is so intense and overwhelming that they, at that moment in time, cannot see any way out of it. In some cases, whatever you may have done or said or may not have done or said, it still may have not made any difference to the way the person was feeling inside and to their choice to take their life.

The person who has died would not want the loved ones left behind to live their lives feeling blame, guilt and bitterness, but would want them to move on with their lives. The person did what they felt was best for them at that time. The people left behind can rationalise that it wasn't the best thing to do, but the suicidal person was at a stage where they could not see that for themselves and may have felt that by ending their life they were saving others around them from hurt and pain. The last thing they would have wanted to do was to cause you more hurt and pain. A person has to find an alternative way out for themselves – if they cannot see that, nobody really has a right to judge them; nobody else is feeling what they felt, nobody else could see what they could see – even if they seemed happy and coping on the outside, nobody could see what they were feeling on the inside. Nobody was living their life but them.

If you have been bereaved by suicide please ensure you get as much help and support for yourself as you can. There is still, unfortunately, some stigma about suicide and it is sad that families and friends of suicide victims often feel they cannot talk about the person who has died in case other people start asking questions and don't understand. It is something that will always be with you so make sure you surround yourself with as much support, love and care as you can so that you don't go through life with this on your own. There are resources on the Internet, helplines and counsellors who will support you and work through your feelings with you.

If you have been bereaved

- Allow yourself to grieve – to express your feelings openly whether they be feelings of loss, anger, guilt, rage, loneliness, numbness, disbelief, confusion etc.
- Don't be afraid to tell others what will help you and what you need – whether it be someone just to listen, someone to talk to about your loved one, someone to look at photos with you, someone just to give you a hug, etc.
- Talk, talk and talk about your feelings as much as you want to – seek support from helplines and counsellors if you feel unsupported, or that others are not there for you in the way that you need them to be.
- If you feel that there are things you wanted to say but didn't then deal with this in whatever way is right for you. Believe that the person has heard and understood what you have said. This should bring you some sense of comfort and peace.
- Try to look after your physical health – you may find difficulty in eating, sleeping etc. but do what you can to look after yourself. The stronger you are physically the more strength you will have to deal with the wide range of emotions you may be experiencing.
- Believe that in time the pain will fade, you will be able to focus more on some of the good memories.
- It may be that you do not feel any real sadness at the death of the person who has died, for example if you did not have a good relationship with that person, or it was someone who caused you considerable hurt and pain. You have no need to feel guilty if you don't feel sad that the person has died – your feelings are your feelings and nobody else's. Nobody else had exactly the same relationship with the person that you had so you have a right to feel however you feel.
- Believe that the person would want you to move on with your life, would want you to laugh, to be happy, to find enjoyment in life.
- Look for new interests, hobbies and friends in order that you don't feel isolated and alone.
- If you find you are becoming very depressed, unable to let go of the person who has died and move on with your life, it may help to seek counselling or to talk to your GP.

Talking to children who have been bereaved

- Allow your child to talk about the person who has died and answer any questions they have as honestly as you can.
- A child may feel that they were in some way to blame for a death (they may have been too naughty, too demanding etc.). Reassure your child that they are not to blame, death is a natural part of life and will happen to everyone at some time.

> ***Believe that in time the pain will fade, you will be able to focus more on some of the good memories***

- Explain to your child that the person who died had no choice in the matter; it does not mean that the person who died did not love them or want to be there for them.
- A child may feel excluded if not included in funeral arrangements and if they are not allowed to attend the funeral – this can actually help a child to accept the reality of death and that the person who has died will not be coming back.
- If a child has difficulty in vocalising how he/she feels encourage your child to draw, write or use toys as a means of expressing how they are feeling.
- Explain to your child that it is okay to be angry, okay to cry, okay to feel lonely – these are all normal feelings to have.
- It may help your child if you ask them if they would like to do something special for the person who has died – this could be planting something in the garden, going down to the coast with you and throwing petals into the sea, making a special book in memory of the person who has died (getting a scrapbook, sticking in photos, writing poems about the person who has died, writing stories about some of the things they had done together, photos of places they went with the person who died etc.).
- If your child talks and makes reference to the dead person, allow them to do that freely.
- It may help at some stage to talk to your child about how to mark the anniversary of the person's death – perhaps go to a special place which the person who died loved to go to and take some flowers. Ask them how they would like to remember the dead person – this may help the child to accept that the person will not be forgotten even though he/she and others need to move on with their lives.
- Your child may want to have some photos of the person who has died to keep in their own room or in a book; this may help comfort them.
- If a child has lost someone very close to them, it may help them to write a diary and to record each day what they would like to say to the person who has died. After a while the child should find that they may not feel the need to write every day and the writing will take place less and less.
- Encourage your child to take up new hobbies and interests, maybe join a group such as Guides, Scouts, St John's Ambulance or the Red Cross, to enable the child to have something else to focus on and take interest in.

■ The above information is reprinted with kind permission from SupportLine. Please visit their website at www.supportline.org.uk for more information, including details of agencies which provide support and information for the bereaved.

Traumatic bereavements

For people affected by natural disasters, terrorist attacks and other traumatic losses

All bereavements are traumatic but some are more traumatic than others. A traumatic loss is one that is unexpected, untimely and often associated with horrific or frightening circumstances.

Whenever a traumatic loss of someone we love takes place, there are four types of problems that may arise:

- Problems of trauma
- Problems of grieving
- Problems of anger and self-reproach
- Problems of change.

We will consider each of these in turn:

Problems of trauma

'I can't believe it's true'

Some bereavements are very hard to take in and make real. This is particularly likely if the loss is unexpected, we have been unable to see or hold the lost person or there is a delay in recovering or identifying them.

What helps?

It takes a long time to take in what has happened and to form a balanced judgement on the basis of the evidence we are given. Spend time talking it through with others and don't worry that you are being a burden to them, that's what friends are for. Many people find it helpful to visit the place where the disaster took place, to talk with others involved, to place a wreath in a significant place and to attend memorial services or other rituals of remembrance. In the end, there may be aspects of the loss that will never be explained. Be prepared to live with the uncertainty of not knowing; we cannot explain or control everything and, fortunately, we don't have to.

Cruse Bereavement Care

'I can't get it out of my head'

Many people are haunted by pictures, in their minds, of the traumatic event. While this is most likely to become a problem if they witnessed the event it can also arise from television or other pictures which 'bring home' the awfulness of the way a person might have died. Such images may occur unbidden or, in distorted form, as recurrent nightmares, or they may be triggered by any reminder of the loss, e.g. loud noises, cries or shouts. So painful are the images that some people go to great lengths to avoid any such reminders. They may shut themselves up at home, avoid talking of the loss, and distract themselves with hectic activity. Although, to some degree, this kind of reaction is not uncommon and will improve with time, in severe form it may become so painful and disabling that it justifies the term 'Post-Traumatic Stress Disorder' (PTSD).

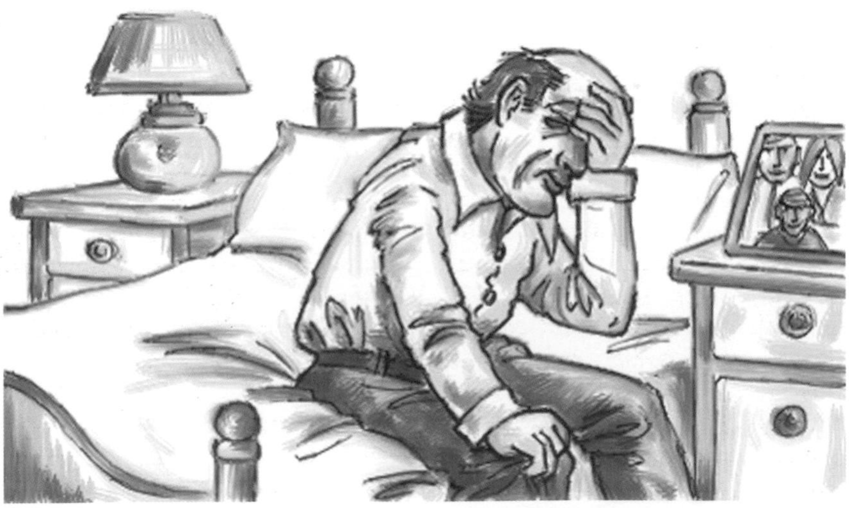

What helps?

Haunting images can sometimes be assuaged by talking to others, going over the events again and again until you get used to them. The images will not disappear but they will become less painful. It becomes easier to live with them. You are back in control. If this is not sufficient to make them tolerable or if the images are stopping you from grieving or getting on with your life, then you should consult a psychiatrist or psychologist. Very effective treatments for PTSD have been developed in recent years and it is unwise not to take advantage of these. They do not necessarily require the prescription of medication although this may help.

Problems of grieving

'I feel numb'

Numbness is our mind's way of protecting itself from mental pain that threatens to overwhelm us. Sometimes it may be so pronounced that we are unable to think clearly, become confused and lose our bearings; at other times we may be unable to express feelings of any kind. In an emergency it is such 'dissociation' that enables us to keep going, searching for a lost person or engaging in the rescue of others. It is only if it continues after the disaster is over that it becomes a problem. Usually this reflects a fear that, if we do not keep our feelings firmly under control, they will take control of us, we shall cry or become a helpless baby.

What helps?

Grief is the natural response to the loss of a loved person. It is more likely to give rise to problems if it is bottled up than if it is expressed. At times of loss it is normal and appropriate to express grief in any way that feels natural. Some people need to cry, others will rage and others just talk endlessly about what has happened. Try to find someone you can trust who will be a good listener and don't worry if, for a while, you look or feel helpless, that will pass. In grieving we do not forget the people we love, we gradually find new ways to remember them. Memories of the past are sometimes painful but they are our treasure, it is best not to bury them for too long. Paradoxically, if we allow ourselves to lose control, for a while, we shall find ourselves better able to live with and to control our feelings.

'I can't stop crying'

Grief goes on much longer than most people expect. We need to recognise that fact and not expect too much of ourselves. This said, there are some griefs which get stuck. Sometimes this reflects our need to punish ourselves – 'Why should I be happy now that he or she is dead?' This is most likely to arise if it is a child who has died, if we blame ourselves for their death or for not being there for them when needed. At other times it reflects long-standing feelings of depression or helplessness, which are easily undermined by a traumatic life event.

What helps?

Grief is not like the measles, we do not go back to being the person we were before our loss. We learn to live with it, and, little by little, the pain will diminish. Grief is not a duty to the dead, those we love would not want us to suffer. Again, talking it through with a friend or a Volunteer from Cruse Bereavement Care will usually help but, if that is not sufficient or we feel perpetually depressed or suicidal, we should not hesitate to seek specialist help. Several treatments including Cognitive Therapies, Psycho-therapies and Anti-depressant medications will be of help and it is worth discussing with your GP which of these alternatives are available in your area and appropriate to meet your needs. Do not give up.

Grief goes on much longer than most people expect. We need to recognise that fact and not expect too much of ourselves

Problems of anger and self-reproach

'I feel so angry'

Anger is a very natural reaction to outrageous loss, particularly if it was caused by terrorism or other human agency. It may be directed appropriately against the perpetrators of the trauma or inappropriately against all authorities or against the people nearest to hand.

In our desperation we may find ourselves hitting out wildly at the people we love the best. Occasionally ill-directed anger may even feed into or bring about a cycle of violence.

What helps?

Remember that anger can be a force for good if it is controlled and directed where it can do good rather than harm. Try to hold back from impulsive outbursts and, if you have said or done things that have hurt others, don't be too proud to apologise. They will understand.

'I blame myself, I feel so guilty'

None of us is perfect and it is easy to seize on something that we did or didn't do in our attempt to find someone to blame for the disaster that has happened. Consequently we end up blaming ourselves. At the back of our minds we may even cling to the idea that, if we punish ourselves, we will make things right again and get back the person we have lost. Sadly this magical thinking is doomed to fail.

What helps?

Sooner or later we have to accept that what has happened is irrevocable and that self-punitive grieving will change nothing. Friends will often say 'You shouldn't blame yourself', and maybe they are right. But we do not choose the way we feel. Guilt and anger are not feelings that can be switched on and off at will. Rather we should try to find a creative use for our grief, to bring something good out of the bad thing that has happened.

Problems of changing

'I feel so frightened'

We all know that disasters happen, but they don't happen to me. Most of the time we go through life with confidence that we are safe, protected from harm and immune from the 'slings and arrows of outrageous fortune'. Then disaster strikes, all in a moment the world has become a dangerous place, we can take nothing for granted, we are waiting for the next disaster.

'My world has been turned upside down'

Fear causes bodily symptoms – tense muscles, racing heart, sweating, breathlessness, sleeplessness – all symptoms which, in the environment in which we evolved, would have helped us to stay alive in situations of danger. But in today's world they do no such thing and are more likely to be misinterpreted as symptoms of illness. This adds to our fears and may set up a vicious circle of fear --> symptoms --> fear.

What helps?

The first and most important thing is to break the vicious circle. Recognise that the symptoms of fear are a sign of normality, at such times a racing heart is a normal heart, headaches, back aches, indigestion, even feelings of panic, are natural reactions that will decline as time passes, they are not symptoms that will lead to something worse. In addition you are not as helpless as you feel. Relaxation exercises, meditation techniques, aromatherapy or whatever makes sense to you will put you back in control.

This said you should not expect to go back to being the secure, confident person that you were before the disaster struck. You have learned the hard way that life is never, and never was, completely safe. You have lost the illusion of invulnerability and will never quite regain it. You are older and sadder as a result. But you are also more mature. You have learned that life has its dark side but that does not mean that you need live your life in perpetual fear. The world today is no more dangerous than it was before the disaster. Previously you had an illusion of safety, the feeling of danger is equally illusory, it will grow less. During World War II this was called the 'Near-Miss Phenomenon'. It affected people who had been closely missed by a bomb, but it passed. Human beings evolved to cope with a much more dangerous world than the one in which we live today. You, and those you love, will survive.

'Life has lost its meaning'

Each person's sense of purpose and direction in life arises from a hundred and one habits of thought, assumptions about the world that we take for granted. 'I know where I'm going and I know who's going with me.' Then, all of a sudden, we can take nothing for granted any more. Perhaps the person who died is the one we would have turned to at times of trouble – and now, when we face the biggest trouble in our lives, they are not there, or, if they are, they are so overwhelmed by their own grief that we cannot burden them with ours. Chaos reigns.

What helps?

Those who have a religious faith may find it helpful to seek pastoral support, others may find spiritual help outside of formal religious frameworks.

When faced with a disaster of this magnitude we must realise that it takes time and hard work to adjust. It is rather like learning to cope with the loss of a limb. For a while we will feel crippled, mutilated, as if a part of ourselves is missing. We feel as if we had lost every good thing that relied on the presence of the person we love for its meaning. But take heart, all is not lost.

Now is the time to take stock of our lives, to ask ourselves, what really matters? When we do that we may be surprised to find that many of the things that made sense of our lives when the lost person was with us continue to make sense of our lives now that they are away. Indeed they may make more sense because they are away. When people say 'He (or she) lives on in my memory', this is literally true.

Bereavement supporters, such as those from Cruse Bereavement Care, who provide counselling after disasters, understand this and will give you the time to talk it all through and find new directions. This will not help you to forget the lost person but to remember them better, and to discover the new meanings that can enrich your life henceforth.

As each one of us grows older, more of our life lies in the past than in the future. As time passes we may come to realise that the future is an illusion, only the past is real! In the long run the most important thing about the people who have died is not how they died, but how they lived. Indeed we may have taken them for granted while they were alive, only later can we see how they fit into the full pattern of our lives. And the meaning is in the pattern.

■ The above information is reprinted with kind permission from Cruse Bereavement Care. Please visit their website at www.cruse.org.uk for more information.

© Cruse

When a parent dies

While it's the natural order of things for people to outlive their parents, knowing that doesn't make it any easier when they die. By Elizabeth Easther

Losing one, or both, of your parents heralds a new stage in a person's development. Many of us, upon finding ourselves at the top of the family tree, feel a stronger than usual urge to be nurtured. So, it's important, when there's been a death in the family and you're taking care of all the arrangements, that you let people take care of you, too.

When my mother died, I thought, at first, that I was coping really well – she'd given me a wonderful life and I helped her to a comfortable, dignified death. But the main reason I didn't fall to pieces was because I couldn't.

Most of all, I needed to be strong for my father, who was obviously suffering the most. It's one thing to

handbag

lose your mum, but how, I wondered, could my sadness compare to that of a man who'd lost the love of his life?

So for me, grief didn't really get a look in – there simply wasn't time amongst helping others cope, dealing with the mail, the calls and the visits – not to mention arranging the funeral, an event one friend likened to a wedding, only with three days to organise it and no idea of numbers.

So how do you cope?

Obviously, there are no easy answers to the question of how you deal with the death of a dearly loved parent. There are no rules or stages for grieving that will suit every person through every loss (although there are scores of books that claim there are) but here are some simple guidelines that were useful to me:

- Sleep – grief is exhausting, but being shattered doesn't mean you'll sleep well. Get help with this if necessary.
- Try to eat a little something – even if you're not hungry. Things will be tough enough without you getting run down.
- Take some exercise – not only is it good for you, but it can also be a useful time to reflect.
- Don't pretend you're not sad – when asked how you are the answer doesn't have to be, 'I'm fine, thanks. And you?'
- Don't feel bad about grieving – sadness, as we all know, is as much a part of life as joy.

Get it write

Beverly lost her mother when she was in her 40s and even then it felt too soon to be left without a mum. 'I missed being able to tell her things . . . you'd think after 47 years I'd have said everything I needed to say, but no, so I started writing to her. Whenever I wanted to speak to her I wrote it down. Little bits of news, things that would've made her laugh, how grateful I was and proud. I'd tell her how much I loved her and missed her and it really helped me. Eventually I wrote less and less and, when I read back over it now, I feel sad but I also feel more connected to her, too.'

Say it now

Thirty-five-year-old Pamela's father died in an accident 12 years ago. She says one of the hardest things was having no warning: 'When people die unexpectedly you really regret things you never said, even though we'd been close. I still have so many questions. Of course I deal with it, there's no choice, but I hate to say that for me, it's got worse rather than better. Life goes on, sure, but this kind of pain doesn't really ease – at least it hasn't for me.'

You don't have to cry all the time

Catherine (31) says laughter helped her cope with her father's death. 'It sounds like something from a self-help book, but finding some humour can be really cathartic. At Dad's funeral, when the hearse was still open, a motorcycle roared past and our family dog freaked and jumped in with the coffin. You couldn't help but laugh, and I think it made us realise that we could laugh, that things were going to be okay.'

How to help

Nothing can really prepare a person for the death of a parent and, because everyone is different, there are no rules. If you want to help someone close to you through this kind of loss, offer them your shoulder, your ears and your love. It's as simple as that.

And finally

When you're able, try to remember the good things about having had that person in your life, not just the sad things about them no longer being there.

And be aware too, deep sadness can come over you at any time, without warning. Assuming you've had a good relationship with your parents, you will miss them always and that's fine because, contrary to popular belief, time doesn't heal all wounds, it just makes some of them a little more bearable.

- Information from handbag.com. Visit www.handbag.com for more.

Pet bereavement

Information from SupportLine

As with any bereavement the death of a much loved pet can be devastating and an enormous loss. To some the pet may have become a member of the family, a companion, a friend – and if you were close to your pet it is normal to have the reactions to its loss that you may experience in the death of a person i.e. shock, disbelief, numbness, anger, pain, hurt, sadness, guilt and overwhelming grief.

> *As with any bereavement the death of a much loved pet can be devastating and an enormous loss*

It can sometimes be hard for others to recognise the extent to which the loss of your beloved pet may be affecting you and it is not uncommon to hear 'it was only a dog' , 'you can easily get another one' etc. As with any bereavement it is important for you to have someone to talk to who does understand exactly how you are feeling and what the loss of your pet has meant to you.

It may be particularly difficult if you were in the position of having to have your pet put to sleep and that is a heartrending decision to have to make. However, making that decision shows the enormous amount of love you had for your pet and the ability you had to put your pet's care and wellbeing before your own thoughts of loss. When a pet we love is ill and suffering, there is no other choice but making the decision to have their life ended with dignity and humanely to end any suffering; your pet would have understood that and the love that you showed him/her by making that decision.

Give yourself time to grieve and remember your pet in whichever way helps – talking, writing, looking at photos. Some people find in time that they want to get another pet but don't rush into this as you need time to get over your loss otherwise it may be something you regret doing too quickly.

However, just as when we lose a person we love they would ultimately want us to move on with our lives and be as happy as we can, it is the same for the pet we have lost – they

too would want us to move on, be happy, remember the good times with them and if it helps to have another pet they would be fine with that too. If you have a lot of love and caring to give to another pet and can give a good and loving home that would be a really good thing to do – when the time is right for you. Don't allow yourself to be pressured into having another pet until you are ready – if you are ready – that is your choice.

There is support for anyone whose pet has died or who has lost their pet in other ways. Please don't feel alone and isolated – there are people who understand and would like to be there to support you in whatever way they can.

Agencies who give support and information

- Pet Bereavement Support Service: 0800 096 6606 – Open every day 8.30am-8.30pm. Will put you in touch with your nearest telephone befriender. www.bluecross.org.uk
- Ease Pet Bereavement Service: Call Angela on 07870 740 605 and she will call you back, www.ease-animals.org.uk
- Animal Samaritans Pet Bereavement Service: 020 8303 1859
- The Association of Private Pet Cemeteries and Crematoria: 01252 844478, www.appcc.org.uk
- SupportLine Telephone Helpline: 020 8554 9004, email info@supportline.org.uk – Emotional support to children, young adults and adults on any issue. Also keep details of counsellors and support groups throughout the UK.

Useful websites

- www.petloss.com – (American site) Grief and loss support
- www.ability.org.uk/pet_loss – Resources relating to pet bereavement, guide to pet euthanasia
- www.pets2rest.co.uk – All aspects of pet bereavement

■ The above information is reprinted with kind permission from SupportLine. Please visit their website at www.supportline.org.uk for more information on this and other issues.

Helping the bereaved

Information from If I Should Die

Many people find coping with bereaved family and friends an awkward and difficult time. Everyone knows the stories of people who would rather cross the street than face what they feel would be a potentially embarrassing conversation with someone who has been recently bereaved.

Make contact

It is very important to make contact as soon as possible. Contact the bereaved person immediately to tell them how sorry you are to hear of their loss. Send a letter or card and flowers if appropriate. Most bereaved people say that reading the letters and cards they receive provides valuable support and comfort, particularly during the many sleepless nights they endure.

You may worry that your words seem rather banal or trite, but they often take on a deeper significance and offer a degree of consolation in the heightened emotions of bereavement. If you know of any words that have particularly touched you, then please let us know via our email.

> *'People use platitudes as a replacement for personal experiences, substituting insensitivity for insight'*

Maintain contact

Keep the contact going with visits, phone calls and letters, particularly as the weeks and months pass by. Often levels of support can fall away in the months after a bereavement, but this is the time when the bereaved can be the loneliest and most vulnerable. Six months is recognised as being a particularly vulnerable time, as it is about this time that the reality of the loss hits home and yet others are assuming that by this stage, people are over the worst.

Continue to invite them to events and functions which you would have previously. They can always say no, but don't make that assumption yourself.

Listen and let the bereaved person talk

Talking is recognised as one of the most important elements in the grieving and healing process. Let

the bereaved person talk about the person who has died and don't be embarrassed by their tears and anger.

Don't use platitudes – Kate Boydell in her excellent website www.merrywidow.me.uk says, 'People use platitudes as a replacement for personal experiences, substituting insensitivity for insight. If in doubt, don't say it.'

> *Consider what practical support you can offer, such as taking a cooked meal, taking care of the children, shopping or helping with any funeral arrangements*

Talk about the person who has died

Many people feel that they shouldn't talk about the person that has died as this will bring on another wave of grief. However, most bereaved people say that they find it hurtful if the deceased is not mentioned, almost as if they had never existed. Remember happy times, things they liked or didn't like, funny things they said. It all helps to keep the memories strong and bring some comfort.

> *Most bereaved people say that they find it hurtful if the deceased is not mentioned, almost as if they had never existed*

Offer practical help

Consider what practical support you can offer, such as taking a cooked meal, taking care of the children, shopping or helping with any funeral arrangements. Try and maintain regular help for as long as needed or possible but try not to make promises that you will be able to keep.

Don't say 'Give me a call if you need anything', help needs to be freely given without the bereaved person having to ask for it – make regular contact and make a date to have the bereaved person/family around for a coffee, Sunday lunch, take the children out, make an extra cake/casserole and drop it round.

Muslim tradition requires that mourners do not cook for themselves for 40 days after a death – relatives and neighbours supply the food.

Be aware of significant dates and anniversaries

Family times such as Christmas and birthdays as well as anniversaries of the death are a particularly difficult and traumatic time for the bereaved and need to be treated with sensitivity, particularly the first few times they come around.

Helpful reading

Waterbugs and Dragonflies by Doris Stickney – Continuum International Publishing Group – Mowbray/August 1997

Specially aimed at children, it helps to explain death through the analogy of the waterbugs' short life under water and their emergence as dragonflies as the human's life after death.

■ The above information is reprinted with kind permission from If I Should Die. Please visit their website at www.ifishoulddie.co.uk for more information.

Helping children

Once adults tried to shield children from death, but modern-day understanding is that avoidance is a recipe for disaster – especially for a child. Like all of us, children need to understand that death is a natural part of life, just as birth is, and two charities in particular are very able to help children, parents and families through the grieving process with professional carers, helpful publications and activities.

Contact the Child Bereavement Trust and Winston's Wish.

Widowhood – A Young Woman's Survival Guide can be found on Kate Boydell's wonderful website – www.merrywidow.me.uk

Kate was widowed at the age of 33 with two young children and her personal experience offers a highly practical, painfully poignant and at times amusing insight into the emotions and experiences of widowhood, from telling her children the news, to coping with DIY.

This is a valuable resource for everyone and is equally useful for those trying to help and understand bereaved family and friends.

Bereavement benefits by number of children

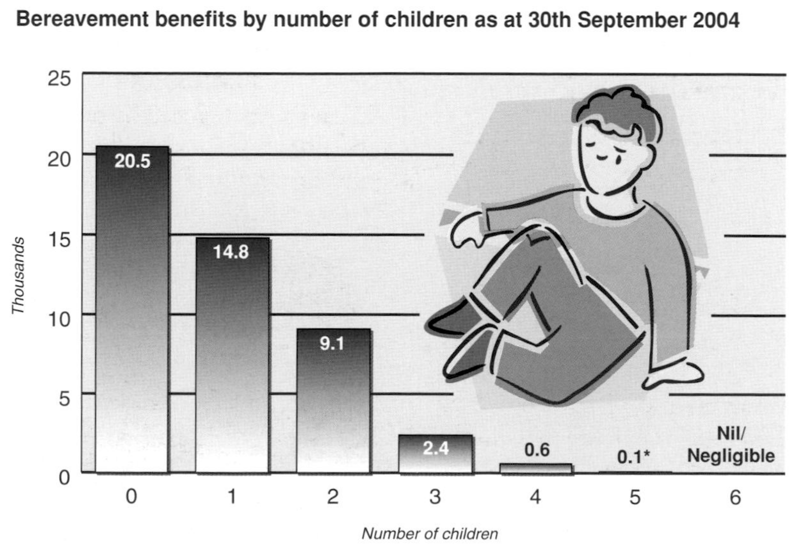

* Figures are subject to a high degree of sampling error and should only be used as a guide

Remembering

Information from the Child Bereavement Trust

Grief is not about forgetting the person who has died, but about finding ways to remember them. Remembering brings healing. When someone dies, our feelings for them and memories of them stay alive and active inside us. We need to find ways of expressing those feelings so that we can move on in our lives, says Julia Samuel, an experienced bereavement counsellor.

When you lose someone important in your life, you may fear you will be unable to conjure up all the happy memories of your life with them. This fear is very common. By taking an active part in creating ways of remembering you can turn those memories into your most prized possessions. This is as true for children as it is for adults.

By taking an active part in creating ways of remembering you can turn those memories into your most prized possessions

Finding ways to remember can help you. There is no right way or wrong way of remembering, nor is this a question of seeking perfection in whatever you have chosen to create. At its best, this process is a deeply personal expression of love for the special person in your life who has died but who lives on in your memories.

The funeral

The funeral is a way of saying goodbye and is also an occasion to look back on and to remember. Because of its importance do make sure you know about the wide range of choices which are available these days. A funeral service no longer needs to follow a fixed format. You can create a ceremony that really expresses the spirit of the person who has died. Take time to consider the options. Whatever you decide, the memory of a beautiful service that felt absolutely right will bring you comfort in the future. Different types of funeral are discussed in detail in separate articles.

Visiting the grave

This can be a way of 'visiting' the person who has died. For many people it is a chance to put the rest of the world aside. You may find that telling them your news, expressing your feelings to them and showing your love through flowers and other gifts becomes an integral part of your mourning.

A memory box

You can make or buy a special box in which to put precious possessions. These could include letters or cards from friends or dried flowers from the funeral.

You could also put into the box treasured things which belonged to the person who has died such as diaries or letters. Ready-made memory boxes often have sections for different keepsakes and a clear plastic cover on the lid for a photograph.

A remembrance book

Creating a book in memory of the person who has died can be a healing process. Include photographs, poems, letters or your own thoughts. In the future the book will bring your memories back to life.

A journal

Writing a diary of your grieving process is useful for a number of reasons. The writing itself is cathartic: putting your feelings into words can help to release some of the pain. Later, you will be able to look back on how you felt and to realise that however bad it was, you survived. That knowledge can help you to realise that whatever you are going through now will also pass. How you use the journal is, of course, up to you – some people sketch, others write down memories, others pour out feelings, yet others do a combination of all of these. You may choose to fill your journal with something entirely original.

Artwork

If you like sewing, stitching a sampler, and framing it can be a lovely option. You could paint a picture and frame that. Making anything in the memory of the person who has died connects you to them and gives you something to treasure.

A candle

Lighting a candle and reading a special prayer or poem can be a simple but powerful way of commemorating an anniversary.

A special walk

One family sent a beautifully illustrated leaflet about a special walk in memory of a little girl. The leaflet showed the route, described the girl and invited anyone who was interested to go on the walk. It was about two miles long, followed roads, went through a wood and ended by a river. Along the way were little hand-carved commemorative plaques with a few lines of a poem or a line drawing. You could create your own special walk.

You can create a funeral ceremony that really expresses the spirit of the person who has died

Planting trees or shrubs

Some people plant a tree or a shrub and have a commemorative plaque set up beside it as a way of remembering. Choose a hardy shrub or tree and make sure you plant it in a place that you will always be able to visit. If you have no place of your own to plant a tree, you may be able to get permission to plant one in a park or other public area.

In memory of

Some families, particularly when a child has died, like to create a charity or a scholarship in their memory – a living memorial to the person. This can be a way of healing the wounds of the person's death. You can invest in a cure for the disease that led to their death, develop their field of interest or continue their work.

Remembrance Service

Many organisations like Cruse and Sands (the Stillbirth and Neonatal Death Society) hold national annual memorial services. Hospitals often hold a remembrance service each year. You can organise your own service for your hospital or an organisation connected with the person who has died. These services are usually very beautiful and enormously appreciated. There is something deeply moving about a group of people from different backgrounds and with different stories coming together in one place to remember the special people in their lives. The service itself is often non-denominational and simple with a few prayers, poems and

hymns, followed by the lighting of candles at the altar by members of the congregation. For some people who have really moved forward in their lives, this service can be the only time they are able to put aside to remember, to feel the sadness again and to be enriched by the memories.

■ The above information is reprinted with kind permission from the Child Bereavement Trust. Please visit their website at www.childbereavement.org.uk for more information.

Mourning sickness feeds the feel-good factor

People who wear ribbons to show empathy with worthy causes and mourn in public for celebrities they have never met are part of a growing culture of 'ostentatious caring which is about feeling good, not doing good'

By Matthew Taylor

People who wear ribbons to show empathy with worthy causes and mourn in public for celebrities they have never met are part of a growing culture

of 'ostentatious caring which is about feeling good, not doing good', according to a study published today.

The report by thinktank Civitas argues that the trend towards public outpourings of compassion reveals not how altruistic society has become, but how selfish.

Author Patrick West said: 'We sport countless empathy ribbons, send flowers to recently deceased celebrities, weep in public over the deaths of murdered children, wear red noses for the starving in Africa, go on demonstrations to proclaim

The study says this 'recreational grief' has replaced institutions like the family, church and neighbourhood

Drop the Debt or Not in My Name ... [but] they do not help the poor, diseased, dispossessed or bereaved.

Our culture of ostentatious caring concerns, rather, projecting one's ego, and informing others what a deeply caring individual you are.'

The study, *Conspicuous Compassion*, says this 'recreational grief' has replaced institutions like the family, church and neighbourhood.

Mr West says: 'We live in a post-emotional age, one characterised by crocodile tears and manufactured emotion ... Mourning sickness is a religion for the lonely crowd that no longer subscribes to orthodox churches. Its flowers and teddies are its rites, its collective minutes' silence its liturgy and mass. But these bonds are phoney, ephemeral and cynical.'

Mr West concludes that instead of 'piling up damp teddies and rotting flowers to show how nice they are' people should try to do some 'unostentatious good'

He says public displays of grief have spiralled out of control in the last decade.

'The traditional two minutes' silence grew to three minutes for the victims of 9/11, five minutes for [murdered teenager] Milly Dowler, five minutes for the Ladbroke Grove crash victims and 10 minutes for an Asian beaten up by white men.

'When a group called Hedgeline calls for a two-minute silence to remember all the 'victims' whose neighbours have grown towering hedges, we truly have reached the stage where this gesture has been emptied of meaning.'

The report by thinktank Civitas argues that the trend towards public outpourings of compassion reveals not how altruistic society has become, but how selfish

The motives of demonstrators who take to the streets to voice their concerns about war, globalisation and third world debt are also questioned.

'The slogan "Not In My Name" is fitting for a generation that comprehends global concerns in terms of choosy consumers,' says Mr West. 'It is a self-important motto for those who regard the world through the prism of passive victimhood.'

Placard-waving demonstrators rarely achieve their goals.

Mr West concludes that instead of 'piling up damp teddies and rotting flowers to show how nice they are' people should try to do some 'unostentatious good'.

'If you do genuinely care about the poor and homeless, try talking to

them ... Don't just wear an empathy ribbon, give money that might help cure life-threatening diseases.

'Most of all, next time you profess that you care about something, consider your motives and the consequences of your words and actions. Sometimes the only person you really care about is you.'

Report details

Conspicuous Compassion: Why sometimes it really is cruel to be kind by Patrick West is published by Civitas, The Mezzanine, 39 York Road, London SE1 7NQ, tel: 020 7401 5470, www.civitas.org.uk @ £8.45 inc. pp.

For more information e-mail CIVITAS on: books@civitas.org.uk or call on (020) 7401 5470.

CHAPTER TWO: GRIEF AND YOUNG PEOPLE

Teenage grief

Things you might want to know

It hurts a lot when someone you love dies. When you are hit by such a disturbing event in your teenage years there is little guidance to help you cope. Remember there is no right way of feeling after someone dies and your feelings are unique to you. No two people experience loss in the same way. This may be the first time in your life that you have faced the death of someone close to you and the turmoil that you might experience can leave you feeling confused and lonely. Grief is the cost of commitment. When someone you have been attached to dies, the feelings of pain and loss are known as grief. Grieving is the process of facing the loss of someone you love.

It is very natural to feel a sense of rage and injustice that the person you love has died

Many people find the subject of death and dying hard to talk about, because it means confronting very difficult issues and emotions. Probably the adults around you are busy, and are struggling with their own grief in their own way. It may be difficult to talk to them and you may feel awkward and not know what to say. Younger brothers and sisters will also be affected by the loss of someone close to them but they too will cope differently from you and you may feel quite alone in your own private pain. But what about you? Life was probably difficult enough before while your relative or friend was ill, but now that they have died, the loss and emptiness can feel overwhelming.

Marie Curie Cancer Care

Devoted to Life

Feelings

Feelings can overwhelm you suddenly and you may want to escape. Your feelings can also make you feel like you are on some kind of roller coaster. In the first few days after the death you may feel numb and empty. You may feel extremely tired or unable to slow down because of nervous energy. Or you may be frightened to be on your own. When someone special dies, particularly if the person is one of your parents, you might go through a whole range of feelings; isolation, guilt, rage and depression, for example.

Anger

It is very natural to feel a sense of rage and injustice that the person you love has died. It is just unfair. Why should this happen to you? You may also feel anger towards the person who has died. Again this is normal and not something else to worry about.

Sadness

You may feel sad and that something is missing from your life. Perhaps you think about how life was and worry about how things are going to be in the future.

You may be unable to concentrate for long or want to be by yourself, resenting other people trying to reach you.

Depression

You may feel there is no purpose to anything any more. You might withdraw from your friends. You feel torn apart. Depression is not a weakness. It's part of saying goodbye to someone you care about. But if you feel overwhelmed by these feelings and they don't seem to be going away, talk to someone you trust.

Loneliness

Being alone is fine. But it becomes loneliness if being alone makes you feel sad and unhappy.

Relief

You can feel a sense of relief for many reasons. Perhaps the person who has died was very ill and suffered a lot of pain or discomfort at the end of their life. Or perhaps you did not always get on very well with the person who has died. It is not unusual to feel a sense of relief.

Guilt and blame

No matter what has happened one of the most troubling feelings is guilt. Regretting things you said or did and wishing that 'if only' things had been different can plague you for a long time afterwards. You may wish you had done more or been more thoughtful. It is very common to feel like this but try to be kind to yourself. People feel guilty for various reasons or they blame themselves in some way.

Tiredness and physical symptoms

Grieving can be emotionally and physically draining. Don't be surprised or alarmed if you feel exhausted and want to sleep more than usual. You are going through an immensely stressful event and our bodies react to stress in different ways, one being by having physical symptoms and illnesses.

Feeling nothing

It is not uncommon to feel nothing at all. You may perhaps have a sense of disbelief and not be able or ready to believe that the person has died.

The funeral

Funerals are important family ceremonies that give people a chance to say goodbye and to cry. Although a funeral is often a sad occasion, it is okay to be sad. Funerals can help you as well. It can be a time when friends and family offer each other support and understanding. If you have never been to a funeral before it might be a good idea to ask someone what will happen and what to expect. You can choose whether to go to the funeral or not.

Remembering

Because of your feelings and the changes that may happen, you will probably spend a lot of time remembering the person who has died, what they gave to you and your life, what they mean to you now that you can look back over their whole life, and how you really feel about them. You get them and their lives in proportion, balance up the good and bad things that you have thought and felt about them. If you want, try writing about the person who has died. A journal or memory-book could be your safe place to get in touch with your feelings.

Or you could make a special photograph album with your favourite photos. Use our activity pack called 'A death in my family' to give you other ideas. Getting on with your life does not mean that you have to forget about the person who has died, or that you are betraying him or her in any way.

Anniversaries

You will have good days when things seem a bit better and bad days when you feel awful. Special occasions such as birthdays or if you have something important of your own to share such as exam results can be particularly difficult times. These will become easier to handle in time.

Who can you turn to for help?

Take things a day at a time and remember your pain and sadness will get better in time but try not to worry if it seems to be taking a long time. You may find there are adults you can talk to. Perhaps a teacher at school, a neighbour or a member of your family or a family friend. Your year tutor at school may be a good listener. You may want to talk to someone from a church, mosque or temple depending on your spiritual beliefs, if you have any. The person who took the funeral of the person you loved may be able to help.

If you feel you can't cope and you are not sure where to turn there are some phone numbers for you on the Marie Curie website. Remember you can always see your own doctor (GP). If you are old enough to go to the surgery by yourself you do not need an adult to make an appointment for you or to go with you unless you wish.

Often you want to be with your friends but they may feel they don't know how to listen or to talk about painful things

Often you want to be with your friends but they may feel they don't know how to listen or to talk about painful things. Sometimes friends want to be helpful but prefer to go out doing things when you desperately want someone to listen to you who is not afraid of your strong feelings. It is also okay to go out – have fun and forget. Knowing other people care can help. If you want to talk in confidence to a professional as a result of someone in your family dying at a Marie Curie hospice there will be someone there to help if you ask.

Many Marie Curie hospices now have their own bereavement worker for children and young people. They will be there to help if you let them know you want to talk to someone.

■ Information from Marie Curie Cancer Care. Visit www.mariecurie.org.uk for more information.

Children and bereavement

Every 30 minutes, the mother or father of someone under 18 dies, which means that:

- approximately two children and young people under 18 are bereaved of a parent every hour of every day in the UK.
- around 50 children and young people are bereaved of a mother or father every day.
- approximately 20,000 children and young people are bereaved of a parent every year.
- 3% of 5- to 15-year-olds have experienced the death of a parent or sibling; this equates to 255,000 young people in the UK.
- 6% of 5- to 15-year-olds have experienced the death of a close friend of the family; this equates to 510,000 children in the UK.
- 13% of 5- to 15-year-olds have experienced the death of a grandparent; this equates to 1,105,000 children in the UK.

Sources

- Wilson, R. (*British Medical Journal 1999*).
- Office for National Statistics; population at mid-2000.
- Meltzer, H, et al, *The Mental Health of Children and Adolescents in Great Britain*, ONS, 1999.

■ The above information is reprinted with kind permission from Winston's Wish. Please visit their website at www.winstonswish.org.uk for more information.

Bereavement – frequently asked questions

Information from Winston's Wish

It happened to me

At Winston's Wish we are very aware that you don't want to be reading this information. You don't want to belong to something with a label of being for 'bereaved young people'. You don't want to be bereaved.

Some people are worried about how they are reacting after the death of someone close. The world seems to have lots of 'shoulds' and 'shouldn'ts' in its head about how young people 'should' react and feel. (For example, 'you shouldn't cry in front of people'...'you shouldn't do that'.) You can see more about this in the article 'Myths about grief' (page 23). You may also be thinking that you have to be 'strong' for your mother's or father's sake and that you should hide how you are feeling.

It is very important to realise that there is nothing 'wrong' with you if you think you are responding to the death differently from other people around you. Everyone will respond in their own way to a death because the relationship you had with that person and the person you are is unique to you. So don't feel that you 'ought' to feel the same way as your parent or your brother or sister.

It is important to remember that no one else has the right to tell you how to feel

One of the most common assumptions made by people who haven't yet experienced the death of a relative or friend is that you must feel sad and weepy all of the time. You may, you may not. It is important to remember that no one else has the right to tell you how to feel.

You are also entitled to have fun, to laugh, to spend time with your friends doing stuff you enjoy if this is what feels right for you.

You may find that you feel as if you are jumping in and out of puddles of grieving – or moving from sunshine to shadows several times a day (or several times an hour).

There is a great need in other people to try and make you feel better so you may have some misguided but well-intentioned person telling you that you will 'feel better soon' or that 'time heals'. If you find that you actually feel worse as time goes on – well, that's pretty normal too, although for almost everyone the day does eventually come when you begin to feel a bit – even if it's only a little bit – brighter.

It happened to someone I know – how can I help ?

Maybe you are looking through these pages for something that will help you support a friend. It's tough to be alongside someone who is grieving and sometimes you can wish yourself somewhere else and doing anything else.

You can also wonder what on earth you can do that will help. Well, the answer is so simple, people don't think it's enough – but if you ask a bereaved person what helps the most they'd say the same thing.

What is this magic answer? Just to be there. Be yourself. Listen if they want to talk. Don't try to cheer them up. Just let them know that you are there for them, however they feel or act.

Sometimes, bereaved people will say they don't want to talk – this doesn't necessarily mean that they will never want to talk. So it can be a great help if you give them the opportunities to talk about the person who has died and about how they are feeling. A simple 'so, how's it going then?' helps.

Sometimes, too, bereaved people become very isolated from their friends – they say they don't want to burden them with how bad they are feeling. What they need then is bags of reassurance that you still want to be their friend. Also, keep the invitations coming – even if for months they all get turned down. The day will come when your friend will be able to say 'yes' again and will be so grateful for your quiet, loyal, steady friendship.

You could suggest that your friend looks at the Winston's Wish website, where they can ask a question or join the message boards.

How often does it happen?

It is estimated that 20,000 children and young people experience the death of a parent each year – one every 30 minutes of every day. Many more experience the death of a brother or sister, a grandparent, aunt or uncle, a family friend. This means that in any group of 100 children and young people aged between 5 and 15, there will be at least 3 people whose parent or sibling has died.

It's important, though, to emphasise that this is something rare – in the group we mentioned above, 97 people will not have to face the death of a loved one before they grow up.

While it is true to say that most people die when they are old (the average life span for a man is 73; the average life span for a woman is 75), terminal illnesses and fatal accidents can affect people of any age.

Does how old you are make a difference to how you grieve?

How we respond to the death of someone important may depend on how old we are when that person dies.

Little children (under 6) may be able to repeat the word 'death' and will be able to tell other people that, for example, 'Daddy is dead' – but they do not understand what 'dead' or 'death' really mean. To say 'Daddy is dead' is about the same as saying 'Daddy is in Denmark' and equally incomprehensible.

It also takes a while before children are old enough to understand that once you die you are dead for ever – it is quite normal for children, on being told for example that Grandpa has died, to ask 'but will he still take me to football on Saturday?' When you think about how often Tom and Jerry recover from being annihilated, it isn't surprising that children tend to think that dead people can just get better.

Older children can understand the permanence of death but haven't yet realised that everyone will die – including their parents – including themselves.

The final pieces of the jigsaw of understanding come when the young person realises that not only old people die – young people can die too if they are ill or have an accident – and that a person is capable of ending their own life.

Some young people – and maybe you are one of these – had to understand this rather too quickly. If your mum, dad, brother, sister or someone equally special has died, you know that death does not only come to old people.

One complication of this growth in understanding is that, if you are bereaved when you are under five years old, you will have a painful journey through the stages of understanding as the reality of the death your family has experienced keeps becoming more and more real to you as the jigsaw of pieces of understanding gets put together.

Will I feel better in time?

You will come across many beliefs about grief. Only you will find out what is true for you and your family – and they may be different things.

You will probably be told that 'time heals' or that 'the first year is the worst'. Some people find this is true – but others find that the second year can be even harder. Or the fourth.

It can be when families and friends ask less about how you are coping or when the invitations fall away or when people assume you are 'over it' that the loneliness and the yearning hits hardest.

Young people have told us that, after a while, their friends stop talking about the person who has died, that teachers no longer ask how they're doing and that sometimes even their own families stop communicating, assuming that it's 'for the best' if the person fades from memory. Yet these young people passionately want to keep talking about the person who has died – they just need some help to do so.

You are entitled to preserve your memories and maintain a connection with the person who has died for as long as you choose.

Should I see the body?

Families, and individuals within families, can have very different views on whether young people should see the body after death.

From our conversations with bereaved young people, we know that you will value the chance to choose but, to make an informed choice, you need information on what is involved.

Families will have different cultural and religious beliefs about seeing the person who has died and attending the funeral, but it can help you to:

- begin to say goodbye
- begin to accept the reality and finality of the death
- begin to understand what has happened
- be less scared.

If you are given the choice of whether to see the person after they have died, some things may help you decide:

- Knowing you can change your mind – at any time.
- Checking that you're happy with the choice you've made – not just because you want to please people.
- Having clear and detailed information about what will happen. ('Aunt Sue and me and you will drive to the Chapel of Rest on the High Street just past the video shop. There's a little room with a few chairs where we can sit and wait. You'll have the chance to change your mind. Then Mr Collins, the undertaker, will come in. He's quite tall and has wispy ginger hair and always wears a suit. Aunt Sue will go in to see dad first.')
- Knowing, quite clearly and in detail, what to expect, ideally from someone else who has already seen the body. ('Your dad is lying in the box called a coffin on a table with his head to the left and his feet to the right. You can see all of him because the lid isn't there. There's a window high up in the wall behind him and you can see a tree through it. Your dad's wearing his old football shirt. There's a rather nice smell from a vase of flowers on the table near your dad's head. He doesn't look quite like Jim as I think of him, partly because he's not jumping up and offering you a drink, and partly because he's got his eyes closed and he's not talking. Partly, I think, because the bit I think of as "Jim" isn't there. It's just his body. So don't be surprised if it doesn't seem to be your dear dad. His skin's cold too. You can touch him. I kissed his forehead which was what I wanted to do but it seemed strange that his skin was cold.')
- Having choices about what to do when you enter the room – for example, you can wait by the door, stroke a head or hand, and leave when you want to.
- You may appreciate taking something with a special meaning to leave with the body, for example, a card you've made, or a shell from a favourite holiday or a picture.

Should I attend the funeral?

Families, and individuals within families, can have very different views on whether young people should attend the funeral.

From our conversations with bereaved young people, we know that you will value the chance to choose but, to make an informed choice, you need information on what is involved.

However, if it will not be possible for you to attend the funeral, for whatever reason, there are other positive ways in which you can be involved. Or, if the funeral happened a while ago, and you regret not attending, it is never too late to have a memorial or other ceremony that includes you in saying 'goodbye'.

Probably the biggest factor that will affect your attendance at a funeral is if you are going to feel your presence is welcome there. Sometimes, funerals can be quite tense as there are a lot of people together who are feeling emotional and may not have seen each other for some time. If there is going to be tension (as opposed to sadness) you'll feel more distressed by the atmosphere than by what is happening. It's your family. You know them best.

It is, however, worth saying that we have spoken to many young people who did not attend the funeral of someone close and later wished they had.

If you have the choice of whether or not to attend the funeral, some things may help you decide:

- Knowing what is involved and how you can be involved.
- Knowing you can change your mind – at any time.
- Checking that you're happy with the choice you've made – and not that you've made it because you want to please other people.
- Having someone you feel comfortable with to act as your supporter for the funeral. This may be an aunt or uncle or one of your best friends.
- Having clear and detailed information about what will happen; this will involve explanations about the difference between, for example, burials and cremations.
- You may be confused by the language people use – it is all of the body of the person who has died that is being buried or cremated. Some younger people wonder what happens to the head, arms and legs.
- Sometimes, people wonder if the person who has died can feel anything. They can't – so they will not feel the flames nor will they be scared at being buried.
- Be prepared for how people will react at the funeral. It can sometimes seem as if people are having a party after someone has died; or it can be upsetting to hear people say: 'How lovely to see you'. This doesn't mean that these people are happy that the person has died – they're just the sort of things that adults say when they meet up. Equally, seeing adults in deep distress may alarm you but this is a reasonable response to the huge thing that has happened.

You are entitled to preserve your memories and maintain a connection with the person who has died for as long as you choose

- Be prepared also for some of the things that adults may say to you. For example, young men may be told that they are the 'man of the house now' and young girls may be told 'they'll all depend on you now'. Remember that you are still a young person and do not have to take on an adult's role.
- Find ways to be involved. This may be in the planning of the funeral service. It may be through saying or reading or writing something about the person who has died. It may be through choosing a particular piece of music. You may wish for something special to be put in the coffin, for example, a picture or something linked to a memory.
- You can still be involved and participate in saying 'goodbye' even if you choose not to attend.

Are there other ways to say 'goodbye'?

It is never too late to hold a memorial or other ceremony for an important person. You could consider linking this to an important date – for example the date of their death, or of the funeral or of their birthday. People who did not attend the funeral may appreciate some of the following ideas; they can also be used for marking the anniversary of the person's death:

- Visit the grave (if there is one – or other special place, for example where the ashes were scattered).
- Visit a place with special memories (for example, the place where you had your best holiday ever).
- Create a special place of your own choosing (for example, in the garden of a new house).
- Visit a place that you went to regularly (for example, the park or the swimming pool) – an everyday rather than a once-in-a-lifetime place.

Some of these ideas may make the occasion special:

- Hold a small ceremony with specially chosen music, poems and tributes.
- Bring a picnic of the dead person's favourite food to share.
- Prepare something to leave in the 'special place' – flowers, a laminated poem, a toy.
- Release helium-filled balloons to which messages are attached on labels. You could say: 'If you came back for five minutes, I would …' or 'I remember when …' or 'My wish for the future is …'
- Light a candle and share special memories with each other.
- Start a collection of memories from family and friends of the person who has died. ('I remember the day Jim got stuck on the school roof after climbing up to get his ball.')

■ The above information is reprinted with kind permission from Winston's Wish. Please visit their website at www.winstonswish.org.uk for more information.

Myths about grief

Information from Winston's Wish

'Children soon forget'

Memories of the person who has died are very precious and are necessary to keep a continuing relationship in place (psychologists would talk about 'continuing bonds' between the person who has died and those who survive). It is important to find ways to feel close to the person who has died. This continuing relationship is a very important part in making it possible to live with grief.

Memories can be preserved in several ways:

- By talking about the person who has died.
- By remembering things you did together.
- By looking at old photographs and keepsakes.

Sometimes, even the nicest people can be terribly embarrassed at knowing what to say after someone has died

- By putting together a 'memory box' of things that remind you of them and the times you were together.
- By writing about them.
- By drawing pictures.
- By lighting a candle on special days.
- By eating their favourite meal on their birthday.

If you don't have specific memories – maybe the person died when you were a baby or maybe you hadn't seen them for a long time – you can still remember the person.

- Ask other people about them – What was their favourite colour? What was their favourite food? Did they like football or tennis or ballet? What was the silliest thing they ever did? What were they like as a young person growing up?
- Put together a memory box or memory store of things connected with the person who has died.
- Put together a 'Family tree' with help from other relatives – it can help to see where the person who died fitted into your family's history.
- Maybe write a letter to them about all the things you wish you'd had a chance to know about them.

Then, when you feel you know them a bit better, you can try some of the ideas above.

'If memories are difficult'

Not all of our memories can be positive ones. You may remember rows, times you shouted at each other, sad days, cross days – even worse… days of pain and misery. You may have a picture in your mind of the person just before they died that's not easy to think about. Or maybe the way they died makes all memories really difficult.

You could try thinking of memories like different sorts of stones – ordinary pebbles, rough rocks and precious stones. The ordinary pebble represents ordinary memories, for example, 'he always had cornflakes for breakfast'. The rough rock represents more difficult memories, for example, the way they died or an argument you'd had. The gemstone represents precious memories, for example, 'we had a brilliant day on the beach and she let me cover her with sand'. There'll come a time when you can hold all three of these stones together in your hand – and, hopefully, all these memories together in your mind.

'It's best not to show children how you are feeling, to keep a "stiff upper lip"'

Some well-meaning people don't seem to understand that it's OK to express how you are feeling in front of young people. There's one old-fashioned school of thought that says that children should never see grown-ups crying. This theory doesn't seem to have any answers to how young people feel if they think they are the only ones who are upset – Do they think the adults don't care? – or do they try to bottle up their own feelings to look like they are 'being good'? One odd thing about this myth is that adults who spend their time trying not to cry in front of their children worry about why their children don't cry in front of them.

Expressing feelings is one way to begin to live with them.

You might be able to help the adults around you if they believe this myth by giving them 'permission' to show how they are feeling too.

'It's kinder not to say anything about the person who's died'

Kinder to who? Sometimes, even the nicest people can be terribly embarrassed at knowing what to say after someone has died. You still hear horror stories of old friends

crossing the street to avoid a bereaved person. The idea that it's better not to mention the death unless the bereaved person mentions it first puts that person into the terrible position of having to start talking themselves – if they really want to talk – or, more often than not, puts them into a place where it's easier to keep silent. And this silence becomes a habit.

Communicating with other people – especially members of the family and those who knew the person who died – is a vital way of remembering and beginning to understand what has happened and how life can go on.

'You're only young – you're not grieving like the adults are'

There are some minor differences in the ways that adults and children grieve. For adults and older teenagers, grief can be more like a river that you have to wade through or drag yourself across. Sometimes, grief feels more like a sea – you're stuck in the middle and you can't even see your way to the other side.

For younger children, grief is more like a puddle that can be jumped into and out from. Sometimes, people misunderstand this and think that because a child is crying one minute and playing a riotous game the next that they are 'heartless' or 'don't care'. This is a myth.

Whatever your age, grief is a horrible feeling – cold, scary, confusing. But it is the normal and natural response to something enormous and terrible – the death of someone close.

'Lots of young people grow up in single-parent families these days – what's the problem?'

There are some similarities and some very important differences between living in families where a parent has died and where a parent has left home through divorce or separation. One of these isn't automatically better or worse than the other – unless, that is, you're in the middle right now.

A parent who has chosen to leave the family home to live elsewhere or with someone else can trigger more anger, lower self-esteem, stronger feelings of rejection, for example,

than a parent who would have given anything to have stayed alive but was killed by illness or accident. However, at least there's the chance that a non-resident parent will walk back in some day – or you can always go and see them.

The difference between the two is 'hope'. The child of divorced or separated parents can hope that a relationship can continue or be reformed at a later date with the absent parent; the child of a dead parent has to live with the reality that they are never ever coming back.

■ The above information is reprinted with kind permission from Winston's Wish. Visit www.winstonswish.org.uk for more information.

What's OK and what's not

Information from the Child Bereavement Trust

You need to know that it is OK to:

- Cry and feel low and depressed. You've lost a great deal.
- To feel angry, embarrassed and not want to talk about your feelings.
- Copy some of the activities and interests your brother or sister had before they died, but you need to retain your own life too.
- 'Live in the past' for a while. It can help you to keep alive the memory of your parent, your brother or sister, but try not to let life pass you by.
- Have fun and enjoy life, to laugh again and forget for a while, forgive yourself for the fights and arguments and nasty things you might have said to your parent, brother or sister who died.
- Go on living.

But it is NOT OK to:

- Use drugs or excessive alcohol to dull your senses. This can only act as an escape and hide the pain, not helping to heal it and it will then take longer to accept the hurt.
- Act out your frustration with reckless driving or skipping school.
- Do things with your anger that can hurt other people because you are hurting yourself.
- Experiment casually with sex, just to get close to someone.
- Hide your feelings and not talk about what is bothering you to protect your surviving parent.
- Act as the scapegoat or bad guy to appear tough.

If you find yourself experiencing some of the following then it is important that you seek extra help:

- Prolonged deterioration in relationships with family and friends.
- Risk-taking behaviour such as drug and alcohol abuse, fighting and sexual experimentation.
- Lack of interest in school and poor academic performance.
- Signs of chronic depression, sleeping difficulties and low self-esteem.
- Dropping the activities that once meant so much to you.

■ The above information is reprinted with kind permission from the Child Bereavement Trust. Please visit their website at www.childbereavement.org.uk for more information.

Questions about death

Questions children may want to ask when someone close to them has died

When someone close to a child dies, for example, a parent or grandparent, the child, like any adult, needs to grieve. Sometimes adults think the best way to protect a child is to avoid talking about the person who has died or about their death. We often find it difficult to talk about death but talking can be an important part of grieving. Just because a child seems to be getting on with their life it cannot be assumed that they are not grieving inwardly. Let your child know that you are there when, and if, he or she wants to talk.

Children cannot be protected from sadness, and losing someone you love is very, very sad. Children are quick to sense an adult's unease and may not feel able to seek the answers to the questions that are troubling them. Therefore, it may help to anticipate some of the possible questions your child may want to ask. If you feel more comfortable talking about difficult issues, then your child will also feel more confident talking about the person who has died and what is happening to themselves or other family members.

Questions about death and what happens afterwards

- What is death?
- Why do people die?
- When do people die?
- Is death for ever?
- What happens after death?
- Do people have a soul?
- What is a soul?
- If death is for ever, how is it that Jesus came alive again?
- What is heaven?
- If Granny is in heaven, why is it that she is buried?
- Can Granny see me from heaven?
- Can I telephone heaven?
- Why can't I put up an extra long ladder to heaven?

What to say?

Usually when people are ill doctors are able to make them well again, but

Marie Curie Cancer Care
Devoted to Life

sometimes the person's body cannot fight the illness, or the person is very old and their body is worn out.

Death occurs when someone's body stops working. It may have been damaged by a bad accident. It may have been damaged by very serious illness or disease. It may just be worn out by old age.

Dying is the process or event that results in a person's death. It is important for young children to be told that when people die nothing can bring them back.

There is a lot we don't know about death. Every culture has different beliefs about what happens after a person dies. People may hold very strong views. But many cultures also share some beliefs. Often people believe that we consist of both a physical body and a soul or spirit. The soul is believed to be the part of us that makes us special and gives us our personality. Sometimes children and adults are comforted by the idea of heaven or a similar place where a person is free from pain and no longer ill. Sometimes children (and adults) can feel angry at God.

The answers you try to give to such questions will depend on your spiritual beliefs. It is all right not to know all the answers, but try to be as honest as you can with your child and try not to be afraid of facing difficult issues that your child wants to raise.

Questions about funerals

- What is a funeral?
- What happens at a funeral?
- What do people wear to funerals?
- Why do people dress up?
- How long does the funeral last?
- Will people cry at the funeral?
- Can I go to the funeral?
- What happens after the funeral?
- What is cremation?
- Will it hurt?

What to say?

It is important to talk to children about the funeral beforehand, especially if they have never been to a funeral before so that they have some idea what to expect. Funerals are special ceremonies usually held in a religious building such as a chapel or church, or perhaps a temple or mosque.

Funerals give everyone who cared about the person a chance to be together to remember the person and are a way of saying goodbye to the person who has died and to celebrate their life.

The body of the person who has died is usually in a coffin, music is usually played and someone speaks about the person who has died. People may bring flowers or make a gift to a particular charity instead.

The body may be buried in the ground or cremated – burned in a very hot furnace or fire. The child needs to know that the burning of the body cannot be seen. The ashes may be scattered in a special place or somewhere which has special memories for you. It is important for a child to know that whatever happens to the body after death, it doesn't hurt – the body cannot feel anything.

Questions about the person who died

- What exactly happened when my Mum died?
- Did you see her die?
- Was she in pain?
- What did the doctor say?

Getting over someone's death doesn't mean forgetting. It just means that you start to feel less upset

What to say?

Not knowing what has happened can make someone else's death even more upsetting and frightening. So it is important to tell children what they need to know in as much detail as they require. This, of course, will vary according to the age of your child and their level of understanding, but never underestimate a child's capacity to understand. Be guided by your child by allowing and enabling them to ask what questions they want.

Questions about me

- Will I die?
- Can I catch cancer?
- Was it my fault?

What to say?

Children may also be frightened that they are going to die too. Knowing the reason that the person died may help to take away some of that fear. Such fears are very real and should never be dismissed. Children often feel guilty – that they somehow contributed directly or indirectly to the person's death. It is very common for a child to feel responsible for a family death. For example, they may believe that if only they hadn't been naughty or made so much noise, or had helped more or loved the person more, the person would not have died.

However, the child needs to know that being naughty does not cause someone else to die and that however kind and loving someone is it cannot stop someone from dying. Similarly the child may have felt angry with the person who has died and wished that they weren't there or didn't take up so much time. It is important for children to know that wishes and thoughts cannot make someone die.

Everyone says and does things that later they wish they hadn't. It is often helpful to concentrate on good memories and happy experiences.

Questions about who will take care of me

- Will my other parent die?
- Will we have to move?
- Will I have to change school?
- Will we have enough money to live on?
- Will we still go on holiday?
- Will I still get pocket money?
- Who will help me with my homework?

What to say?

After the death of a parent, children may fear that their other parent or the person looking after them may die too – especially if the other person becomes ill. Young children may believe that all illnesses have the same outcome; reassurance can be very helpful. If a child is afraid to go to school it may be helpful to contact the school and talk to their teacher. Perhaps they would allow extra phone calls during the day, for example, so that the child has a plan and feels more in control. Children may worry about how their family will manage financially or whether they will need to move house or school.

Often there will be quite major changes for a child following the death of a close family member. It is best to be honest with your child. Children may not like what you tell them but most will prefer to know rather than to guess and worry about things. It may be that the news is better than they expect. Children need to feel emotionally secure as well as physically safe, so make sure that they know you will be there for them.

Questions about the future

- Will my sad feelings go away?
- Will I ever feel happy again?
- Can I go to the cemetery?
- Can I make a special card to take to the cemetery?
- Will we be together when I die?
- Will I forget my Mum?

What to say?

Getting over someone's death doesn't mean forgetting. It just means that you start to feel less upset. You do not forget the person who has died but you find a way of giving them a new place in your life and your memories.

It is important that your child does not feel he or she is betraying the person who has died by getting on with their life.

It will probably be helpful to mark anniversaries in some special way, perhaps monthly at first and then each year. Perhaps your child would like to make a card or pick a flower to take to the cemetery or garden of remembrance. It is often a good idea to let your child choose something that belonged to the person who has died as a memento. You may want to share activities that remind you of the person who has died perhaps by doing some of the things suggested in the activity pack available from your Marie Curie Hospice.

■ The above information is reprinted with kind permission from Marie Curie Cancer Care. Visit www.mariecurie.org.uk for more information.

Better help urged for bereaved young people

Information from the Joseph Rowntree Foundation

'I just can't get over it at times…when it's really hard, it's like losing a part of yourself…it's like learning to walk again…' Neville, 19, interviewed a year after witnessing his mother's sudden death from a heart attack.

JOSEPH ROWNTREE FOUNDATION

Young people who experience the death of someone close to them – whether a parent, brother, sister, grandparent or friend – should be offered better support to help them grieve and cope with potential long-term consequences of their loss. A range of provisions, from 'death and bereavement' education in schools to peer support and specialist counselling, could be made widely available, according to a study for the Joseph Rowntree Foundation.

The report argues that it is more common for children to encounter the death of a close relative or friend than is often appreciated. Research suggests that between 4 and 7 per cent of young people may lose a parent before age 16, and that a similar proportion experience the death of a sibling – most often the loss of a baby brother or sister.

However, one survey found that more than nine out of ten children and young people have experienced the death of someone 'close' or 'significant' to them, such as grandparents and friends (and sometimes including much-loved pets). Other research suggests that large numbers of bereaved young people never talk to anyone about their experiences, with a risk of growing social isolation.

Reviewing the evidence, Jane Ribbens McCarthy of the Open University and Julie Jessop of Cambridge University conclude that the help available to young people through schools and bereavement organisations is patchy, and highly variable in quantity and content. They argue that particular attention should be paid to support services in disadvantaged areas that have the highest mortality rates.

Dr Ribbens McCarthy said: 'Bereavement can have particularly harmful implications for young people who are already vulnerable or living in disadvantaged circumstances. The many difficulties in their lives put them at particular risk of poor mental health and other problems following their loss. A variety of support services ought to be available so that all bereaved young people can access help, if and when they want it. These range from basic information to individual and family-based programmes, including provision for bereavement in particular circumstances, such as sudden, accidental death or suicide.'

In calling for better support services, the report acknowledges that young people respond in different ways to the death of someone close to them; and it accepts that they will not necessarily welcome or need 'expert' help. For some, friends and families may provide the key supports, but others may experience bullying by their peers, and alienation – even outright abuse – from other family members.

The study also notes that while many bereavements are deeply upsetting and can have sustained, adverse effects on children, not all the consequences are necessarily negative. One young woman, quoted in the case studies, described how the death of her great-grandfather had brought her closer to her family and made her aware of the need to 'get on' with life.

Looking at bereavement as a 'risk factor' for long-term problems, the report reviews a large number of research studies, whose findings are often contradictory. For example, some researchers have identified higher than expected levels of disruptive behaviour among children that have lost a parent, while others conclude the link is minimal or non-existent. There are comparable disagreements over how far childhood bereavement is associated with depression and other mental health problems. More, and better, research is needed into such issues.

It is, nevertheless, clear that young people who experience several bereavements, or other losses, during childhood are at increased risk of long-term emotional and social problems. The evidence also shows that the chances of experiencing multiple losses among family and friends are related to deprivation and living in a disadvantaged area.

Dr Ribbens McCarthy said: 'We need to understand bereavement as something that most young people will experience while they are still growing up. Although many find ways of their own to cope, without the need for "expert" help, the evidence suggests that the loss of someone close to them often holds long-term significance in their lives. The notion that children and young people will simply "get over it" can be especially unhelpful.'

15 June 2005

■ The above information is reprinted with kind permission from the Joseph Rowntree Foundation. Visit www.jrf.org.uk for more information.

A checklist

What to do when someone dies

When someone dies, certain people and organisations need to be told and certain documents completed. Some of these things can be done by a close relative or friend; others need to be done by the executor or administrator of the deceased's estate. This information applies to England and Wales only.

What to do in the first five days

You cannot be expected to do everything right away, but in the first five days it's important that you:

- notify the family doctor
- register the death at the Registry Office
- contact a funeral director to begin funeral arrangements (you'll need to check the will for any special requests – the deceased's solicitor may have a copy if you can't find one)
- if relevant, complete form BD8 and send to the local Jobcentre Plus or Social Security Office (given to you when you register the death; read the reverse to see if it applies)
- if the person who has died was receiving any benefits or tax credits, advise the offices that were making the payments

You should also:

- contact the executor if this isn't you (usually nominated in the will to sort out the deceased's affairs) – to enable them to start the process of obtaining probate
- if there is no will, decide who will apply to sort out the deceased's affairs and contact the Probate Registry to apply for 'letters of administration'.

Who else to contact as soon as possible

As well as informing people who are close to the deceased, in many cases you'll need to close down accounts, or cancel or change insurance details, subscriptions, agreements, payments or direct debits.

...SHE'S NOT HERE RIGHT NOW... THAT'S WHY I'M PHONING...
SK

The personal representative looking after the deceased's affairs will also need to check the value of any insurance or pension funds, savings accounts and similar and arrange payment of insurance/ pension benefits and any outstanding tax or debts before distributing the remaining estate to beneficiaries.

- relatives and friends
- employer
- school
- solicitor/accountant
- the deceased's Tax Office
- National Insurance Contributions Office if they were self-employed (to cancel payments)
- Child Benefit Office (at latest within eight weeks)
- landlord or Local Authority if the deceased rented
- Local Authority if the deceased paid Council Tax, had a parking permit, and/or received social services help, attended day care or similar
- any private organisation/agency providing home help
- general insurance companies – contents, car, travel, medical etc. (if the deceased was the first named on an insurance policy, make contact as early as possible to check that you are still insured)
- Pension providers/Life insurance companies
- Bank/building society
- mortgage provider
- hire purchase or loan companies
- credit card providers/store cards
- utility companies if accounts were in the deceased's name
- TV/Internet companies with which the deceased had subscriptions
- any other company with which the deceased may have had rental, hire purchase or loan agreements

- Royal Mail, if mail needs re-directing
- Deceased Preference Service and Bereavement Register to remove the deceased's name from mailing lists and databases
- UK Passport Agency, to return and cancel a passport
- DVLA, to return any driving licence, cancel car tax or return car registration documents/ change ownership
- clubs, trade unions, associations with seasonal membership for cancellation and refunds
- Church/regular place of worship
- social groups to which the deceased belonged
- dentist
- creditors – anyone to whom the deceased owed money
- debtors – anyone that owed the deceased money.

Claiming benefits if you lived with or were dependent on the deceased

Depending on your income and circumstances, you may be able to claim certain benefits if you lived with or were dependent on the deceased. Time limits apply, so check the details as early as is possible.

Bereavement and funeral benefits
Make a claim for Bereavement Allowance, Widowed Parent's Allowance and/or the one-off Bereavement Payment if you are widowed or become a surviving civil partner (time limits apply).

Claim a Funeral Payment to help with funeral costs if you're on a low income.

> *You may be able to claim certain benefits if you lived with or were dependent on the deceased*

Claiming other benefits or reporting a change of circumstance
Check whether there are other benefits you can claim, or whether your current benefits need to change.

If you were living with or dependent on the deceased, any current benefits you are receiving may change, or you may be able to claim additional benefits. To check your entitlements, contact your nearest Jobcentre Plus office, or read the Department for Work and Pensions (DWP) leaflet *What to do after a death in England or Wales*.

- Information reprinted with permission from DirectGov. Visit www.direct.gov.uk for more.

When someone dies

Things people say when someone dies

How you respond to a death of someone close to you will be very individual and personal. These are some of the things people often say when someone dies. They may help you to feel that you are not completely alone or to understand what someone you know is going through.

I can't believe it
It may take you a long time to grasp what has happened. Some people carry on as if nothing has happened. It is hard to believe that someone important is not coming back.

I feel nothing
The shock can make you numb, you may feel you're in a different world.

Why did this have to happen?
Death can seem cruel and unfair, especially when you feel someone has died before their time or when you had plans for the future together.

I feel such pain
Physical and mental pain can feel completely overwhelming and very frightening.

I go over it again and again
You can't stop thinking about the events leading up to the death.

If only...
You may feel guilty about things you said or did or that you didn't say or do.

I feel so depressed, life has no meaning, I can't go on
Many people say there are times after a death when they feel there is nothing worth living for and they feel like ending it all.

I hear and see her, what is wrong with me?
Thinking you are hearing and seeing someone who has died is a common experience and can happen when you least expect it.

They said I'd be over it in a few months
Many people find it takes much longer to learn to cope without someone they love.

One minute I'm angry and the next minute I can't stop crying
Many people find they experience mood swings which are very frightening.

- The above information is reprinted with kind permission from Cruse Bereavement Care. Visit www.rd4u.org.uk for more information.

After a death

What to do initially

If the death occurs at home

Expected death

If the cause of death is quite clear and the doctor had attended the deceased during their last illness he or she will give you the following:

- a medical certificate that shows the cause of death (this is free of charge and will be in a sealed envelope addressed to the registrar)
- a formal notice which states that the doctor has signed the medical certificate and tells you how to get the death registered.

If the body is to be cremated, the doctor will arrange for the signature of a second doctor required to complete the cremation certificate. Doctors charge fees for providing cremation certificates.

In a few cases, the doctor may report the death to the coroner.

If it was the wish of the dead person or their nearest relative that the body or organs should be donated for transplant or medical research purposes, the doctor will have to be contacted quickly. Organs cannot normally be used when death occurs at home, but the body can still be donated to medical science.

You may wish to contact the deceased's minister of religion if you have not already done so. Arrangements for laying out the body and organising the funeral can be made by a funeral director.

Unexpected death

If you discover a body or the death is sudden or unexpected, you should contact the following people (if known):

- the family doctor
- the deceased's nearest relative
- the deceased's minister of religion
- the police, who will help find the people listed above if necessary.

If the death was violent or accidental, or if there are unusual circumstances or the cause of death is not known for certain, or there is any reason to suspect that the death was not due to natural causes, contact the police immediately. Do not touch the body or anything nearby, or remove anything from the area. The death may be referred to the coroner.

If the death occurs in hospital

If the death occurs in hospital, the hospital staff or the police (if death was accidental) will contact the person named by the deceased as next of kin. This may be, but need not be, a relative. If you have been named as next of kin they will arrange a convenient time for you to attend the hospital. You will then be asked to:

- identify the body;
- give permission for a post-mortem in cases where there is no legal requirement but doctors think that it is advisable in order to establish a cause of death.

Hospital staff will arrange for the nearest relative to collect the deceased's possessions. If you know that the person wished to donate their organs after death, you should let the hospital staff know, but it is more likely that they will approach you if the circumstances are likely to favour organ donation. You should also let the staff know if the body is to be donated to medical science.

You may, if you wish, request to see the hospital chaplain. The hospital will keep the body in the hospital mortuary until the executor arranges for it to be taken away.

The hospital will:

- either issue a medical certificate of cause of death needed by the registrar, provided the cause of death is quite clear. There may be a post-mortem provided the nearest relative agrees;
- or, in a few cases, report the death to the coroner and make arrangements for a post-mortem if required.

If the actual time of death is not known, the doctor may estimate the time of death.

Registration

By law all deaths occurring in England and Wales must be registered. A death should be registered as soon as possible to allow funeral arrangements to go ahead.

Since 1 April 1997 a death can be registered at any registrar in England and Wales (the procedures differ slightly in Northern Ireland – see below). You do not have to go to the registrar in the district where the death occurred, or where the deceased person lived, although it is usually more convenient to register a death in the sub-district in which it happened. You can find the address in the phone book under Registration of Births, Deaths and Marriages, or from the doctor, local council, post office or police station. Check when the registrar will be available and whether only you need to go along. It may be that someone other than you will be needed to give information for the death to be registered.

If the death has not been referred to the coroner, go to the registrar as soon as possible. The death must be registered within five days (unless the registrar says this period may be exceeded). The declaration will then, if appropriate, be forwarded to the registrar for the sub-district where the death took place, where it will be registered. There may be some delay in certificates being issued, as this cannot be done until the death has been registered.

Reporting a death to the coroner

The doctor may report the death to the coroner if it resulted from or occurred in any of these circumstances:

- the deceased was not attended by a doctor during the last illness or the doctor treating the deceased had not seen him or her either after death or in the 14 days before the death
- the death was violent or unnatural or occurred under suspicious circumstances
- the cause of death is not known or is uncertain
- the death occurred while a patient was undergoing an operation or did not recover from the anaesthetic
- the death was caused by an industrial disease
- the death occurred in prison or in police custody.

The coroner may be the only person who can certify the cause of death. The doctor will write on the formal notice that the death has been referred to the coroner.

The coroner

The coroner is a doctor or lawyer responsible for investigating deaths.

If you want advice or information about a death which has been reported to the coroner, contact the coroner's officer. You can get the address from the police station or, if death was in hospital, the hospital official dealing with deaths.

Coroner's post-mortem

The coroner may arrange for a post-mortem examination of the body. The consent of the relatives is not needed, but they are entitled to be represented at the examination by a doctor.

If the post-mortem shows that death was due to natural causes, the coroner will issue a notification by the coroner (the pink form 100), which gives the cause of death so that the death can be registered. The coroner usually sends the form direct to the registrar, but may give it to you to deliver.

If the body is to be cremated the coroner will give you the certificate for cremation (form E) which allows cremation to take place.

Coroner's inquest

An inquest is an inquiry into the medical cause and circumstances of a death. It is held in public, sometimes with a jury. It is up to the coroner to organise the inquiry in a way to best serve the public interest and the interests of the relatives.

The coroner will hold an inquest if the death:

- was violent or unnatural
- was caused by an industrial disease
- occurred in prison
- or if the cause of death remains uncertain after post-mortem examination.

Coroners hold inquests in these circumstances even if the death occurred abroad (and the body is returned to Britain). If a body has been destroyed or is unrecoverable a coroner can hold an inquest by order of the Secretary of State if death is likely to have occurred in or near a coroner's jurisdiction.

If an inquest is held, the coroner must inform, amongst others, the following people:

- the married partner of the deceased
- the nearest relative (if different)
- the personal representative (if different from above).

Relatives can attend an inquest and ask questions of witnesses, but they may only ask questions about the medical cause and circumstances of the death.

It may be important to have a lawyer to represent you if the death was caused by a road accident, or an accident at work, or other circumstances which could lead to a claim for compensation. Legal aid for representation at inquests is only available in exceptional circumstances.

If the enquiries may take some time, ask the coroner to give you a letter confirming the death. You can use this letter for Social Security and National Insurance (NI) purposes.

The coroner may give you an order for burial (form 101) or a certificate for cremation (form E) so that the funeral can take place. This can usually be done before the inquest is completed, provided the body is not required for further examination.

The coroner will also send a certificate after inquest (form 99 (rev)), stating the cause of death, to the registrar. This allows the death to be registered.

The preliminary arrangements

You will need to decide:

- where the body is to rest while awaiting the funeral
- the time and place of the funeral
- how much you intend to spend on the funeral
- whether to have a funeral service
- whether to have flowers, or to make any donations to a named charity
- whether to put a notice in the newspapers
- whether the body should be buried or cremated.

Check the will to see if there are any instructions for the funeral left by the deceased. It is generally up to the executor or nearest relative to decide whether the body is to be cremated or buried. The executor does not have to follow the instructions about the funeral left in the will.

The funeral director will help you to decide where the body should stay until the funeral, and the starting point, time and place of the funeral. See the funeral directory of UK homes on the If I Should Die website.

If there is to be a service or ceremony, contact the appropriate person for the religion or belief concerned. If you are not sure what to do or who to contact, the funeral director should be able to help you. You can choose the place for the funeral service and you may be able to choose the person to conduct the service. You do not have to hold a religious service. If you wish you can design your own non-religious service.

You also need to decide whether you want flowers for the funeral, or perhaps donations to a named charity. If you want flowers and a cremation is planned, you can decide what should be done with the flowers. The local hospital or old people's home may be pleased to accept cut flowers.

- Information from UK Funerals Online. Visit www.uk-funerals.co.uk for more information.

Religious traditions

Information from If I Should Die

The six recognised world religions all mark the important events in a person's life such as birth, marriage and death in different ways, but there are often similar concepts. Death sees the close of a human life on earth, and the ritual and beliefs linked to death and the funeral, are an important way for the family and friends of the deceased to express their grief and acknowledge the passing. It is often seen as an opportunity to celebrate somebody's life and mark their transition to another life or stage, whatever that may be.

There are also alternative ceremonies available that are not associated with traditional religions, one of the most well-known is the humanist movement.

Christian funerals

- The name Christian actually covers a broad variety of cultures, crossing all continents. In the UK it is estimated that there are up to 220 different Christian denominations, and funeral rituals may differ from church to church.
- Essentially, the Christian belief is one of resurrection and the continuation of the human soul, which stems from a trust in the death and resurrection of Jesus Christ as a way to everlasting life.
- Many people call themselves 'Christian' but may not be actively linked with a church, and some churches may decline to hold a funeral service for someone who has not been an active member.
- Many churches have specially written funeral services, as well as special readings, prayers and hymns (songs). These will include readings from the holy book, the Bible.
- Some funerals may include a special service called Holy Communion, Eucharist or Mass which recalls the last supper that Jesus Christ shared with his disciples before his death.
- At the end of the service, special prayers are said either when the mourners are standing around the grave or if it is a cremation, when the coffin disappears from view.
- It is traditional to wear dark clothes to funerals and black ties with suits, but sometimes, people prefer to wear bright clothes as a celebration of life and resurrection.
- Some funeral services may be followed later by a memorial, particularly if the family prefer a simple, private funeral. The memorial service provides the opportunity to celebrate the life of the deceased with a wider group of friends and colleagues.

Jewish funerals

- Jewish funerals are governed by a set of rituals and traditions which particularly apply to the seven immediate family members; the spouse, mother, father, son, daughter, brother or sister.
- Some of the rituals may differ according to the different Jewish communities. Sephardi Jews originate from Spain and the Middle East and Ashkenazi Jews originate from Eastern Europe and Russia. Whilst Sephardi Jews have a strong communal bond, Ashkenazi may be divided into Orthodox, Conservative and Reform communities.
- Every Jewish community has a burial society called a Chevra Kadisha who prepare the body for burial and help make the funeral arrangements.
- Jewish burials are usually held within 24 hours of death, but may be delayed if immediate family members have to travel long distances.
- Most Jews are buried in a cemetery and some communities consider cremation a desecration of the body.
- At the cemetery, the family and friends congregate in a small chapel with the coffin.
- A symbolic small tear (Keriah) may be made in the mourner's clothes which represents a broken heart.
- A eulogy (hesped) is given by the rabbi or close family friend.
- The Kaddish, an ancient prayer, is recited in Hebrew and again after the coffin has been interred.
- The coffin is taken to the gravesite and it is considered an honour to help shovel in the earth.
- There is a symbolic washing of hands by everyone and everyone returns home.

- In the evening, the first shiva will take place. This is the time when the mourners stay at home and will be visited by friends and acquaintances. A year of official mourning follows and certain communities will have specific customs associated with the year.

Hindu funerals

- For Hindus, death represents the transition of the soul from one embodiment to the next and is the means by which the spirit can ascend its journey towards Heaven or Nirvana.
- Hindus believe in reincarnation and a Hindu funeral should be as much a celebration as a remembrance service.
- Hindus cremate their dead and the burning of the dead body signifies the release of the spirit. The flames themselves are important as they represent the presence of the god Brahma, the creator.

- The vast majority of Hindus come from the Indian continent and it is often an area of regret that a loved one has died far away from their homeland and its traditions.
- As with all religions, ritual plays an important part. Ideally a Hindu should die while lying on the floor, in contact with the earth. Family members will perform prayers and although touching the corpse is considered polluting, many mourners will need to do so to say farewell.
- White is the traditional colour and mourners will usually wear traditional Indian garments. If you are attending the funeral of a Hindu friend, it may be as well to ask what is appropriate to wear.

The six recognised world religions all mark the important events in a person's life such as birth, marriage and death in different ways

- Prayers are usually said at the entrance to the crematorium and may be offered enroute. Offerings such as flowers or sweetmeats may also be passed around and noise is also part of Hindu rituals, which may include horns and bells.
- The chief mourner, usually the eldest son or eldest male in the family, represents the whole family in saying goodbye to the deceased. They and sometimes all the male members may shave their heads as a mark of respect.
- Scriptures are read and then the chief mourner will push the button to make the coffin disappear, as well as going below to ignite the cremator.
- After the cremation, the family may come together for a meal and prayers and begin a period of 13 days' mourning, when friends will visit and offer condolence.

Sikh funerals

- Founded in the 15th century, the Sikh religion has its origins in traditional Hindu beliefs but has its own teachings and central scriptures which lay down many of the traditions associated with death and funeral rites.
- While rejecting the theory of rebirth, Sikhs believe in an afterlife, when the soul meets with the supreme soul, God (Akal Purakh).
- Cremation is the traditional method of disposal of the body, although other methods may be acceptable.
- It is usual to go to the house of the family before departing for the crematorium and the body may be on display.
- Death is seen as an act of the Almighty and it is written in the scriptures that emotions should be kept under control, so family members may appear detached.
- On the way to the crematorium, hymns may be sung and once there prayers may be recited and more hymns sung.
- The next of kin usually will press the button for the coffin to disappear.
- The ashes are normally scattered in the sea or running water.
- After the cremation, guests usually return to the family home where there will be more readings and hymns.
- The mourning period usually lasts between two and five weeks during which time other ceremonies may also be held.

Islamic Funerals

- There are two major groups of Muslims – Shi'ite Muslims and Sunni Muslims.
- Funeral traditions tend to have developed over the centuries, rather than being set out in the religion's holy book – The Koran.
- Muslims try to bury the body within 24 hours of death if possible. They believe that the soul departs at the moment of death.
- The deceased is placed with their head facing the Muslim holy city of Makkah.
- Ritual washing is performed usually by family members or close friends, usually according to the sex of the deceased.
- The body is wrapped in a shroud of usually simple, white material.
- Afterwards, salat (prayers) will be said for the deceased.
- Funerals should be kept simple and respectful and it is forbidden to cremate the body of a Muslim.
- Muslims are buried with their face turned to the right, facing Makkah, and it is customary not to use a coffin.
- Mourners may throw earth onto the coffin in the grave. The grave may be raised above ground level and any gravestone should be simple.
- There is an official mourning

period of three days (longer for a remaining spouse) and this may include a special meal to remember the deceased.

Buddhist funerals

- It is estimated that there are up to 570 different varieties of Buddhism. There are few formal traditions relating to funerals and they are essentially seen as non-religious events.
- The simple approach and emphasis on the person's state of mind leading up to death have led to a marked increase and interest in Buddhist funerals in the West.
- Most Buddhist schools of thought concentrate on the spirit or mind of the deceased and agree that the physical body is just a shell. Many also share the Tibetan belief that the spirit of the deceased will undergo rebirth, usually after a period of 49 days.
- Cremation is the generally accepted practice in Asia – the Buddha himself was cremated.
- A simple service may be held at the crematorium chapel at which Buddhist readings may be recited.
- For a more formalised ceremony contact Throssel Hole Priory which is a Soto Zen Buddhist monastry with a small cemetery attached. Telephone 01434 345 204 (9am -12 noon and 2-4pm).

Humanist funerals

- Humanist organisations exist worldwide to serve the needs of the non-religious, evolving as those needs change. The British Humanist Association (BHA) developed from the Ethical Union in 1967.
- Humanists are non-religious people who live by moral principles based on reason and respect for others, not obedience to dogmatic rules. They promote happiness and fulfilment in this life because they believe it is the only one we have.
- Humanist non-religious funeral ceremonies acknowledge loss and celebrate a life without employing religious rituals. They offer a dignified alternative to the traditional funeral service and are made memorable by being personally tailored to each individual situation, with the wishes of the family taken fully into account. A typical ceremony will usually include:
- Favourite or appropriate music (of any kind).
- A welcome and a brief explanation of the ceremony.
- Poetry or prose readings.
- A 'tribute' to the deceased, mainly biographical, often with short contributions from family, friends and colleagues.
- A time of reflection for silent meditation or private prayer
- The Committal or words of farewell.
- A brief close, which can include thanks and announcements.
- Prior to the funeral, a Humanist officiant will normally visit a family to map out the ceremony and to form a rounded picture of the subject. At this stage it may also be important for families to freely discuss various options in relation to procedure during the ceremony.
- Detailed preparation prevents reliance on a standard text or format, and in the days leading up to the ceremony time and care is devoted to writing and compiling a tribute both factually accurate and with the appropriate tone. By this process, each ceremony can be developed afresh with families who welcome the opportunity for choice and personal input. A printed copy of the ceremony is always provided for the family, to send to absent relatives or friends and kept as a memento.
- Humanist funeral ceremonies may be conducted at crematoria, cemeteries, woodland burial grounds, and other burial grounds (subject to restriction).
- Memorial ceremonies are more usually conducted elsewhere and after some time has elapsed following the funeral. However, in some circumstances, for example where there is no body or a body has been accepted for medical research, a memorial ceremony may take the place of a funeral.
- All Humanist officiants are non-judgemental, empathic and have wide life-experience; many have professional backgrounds. They are accredited by the British Humanist Association, 1 Gower Street, London WC1E 6HD. Tel: 0207 079 3580. www.humanism.org.uk

- Information reprinted with permission from If I Should Die. Visit www.ifishoulddie.co.uk for more.

Alternative burials

Coffins are so last century for Britons seeking life after death

By Mark Honigsbaum

Remains embedded in an 'eternal reef' and towed out to sea; ashes placed in a capsule and launched into orbit; 'cremain' paintings in which a deceased's cremated remains are mixed with oil paint and daubed on giant canvases.

A group of experts on death and dying yesterday disclosed some of the unusual methods of disposal which people are requesting for their own remains. Thumbies for instance – charms fashioned from impressions taken from a deceased person's fingerprints or, in the case of a beloved pet, paw marks.

'These days death has become just one more challenge, another project like our obsession with our bodies'

Glennys Howarth, the head of Bath University's social and policy sciences department and the organiser of yesterday's conference, said the taboo on death was a thing of the past.

She said: 'As society has become more secular and cremations have replaced burials in popularity, that has changed. These days death has become just one more challenge, another project like our obsession with our bodies.'

Our fascination with death is reflected not only in the boom in cremation mementos but in the rise of roadside memorials, books of condolence and offerings of floral bouquets following major disasters such as September 11 and the recent attacks on London.

It also manifests itself in TV programmes such as *Six Feet Under* and *CSI:Crime Science*, as well as the popularity of 'cyberspace cemeteries' – websites where family and friends can leave virtual messages for the dead.

The theme running through all of these phenomena, says Ms Howarth – who is planning to set up a Centre for Death and Society at Bath to study these trends and offer policy advice to politicians – is that death is no longer considered the end of the story.

'With burial you are placed in a coffin in the earth and that's it, you can't move. But now that society has become more mobile we are looking for ways that we can move on and persist after death too,' she said.

George Dickinson, a sociologist at the College of Charleston, South Carolina, agrees. With an estimated 77 million American baby boomers reaching the age of 50 between 1966 and 2015, he predicts that dying will soon become a major obsession.

He says Americans prefer burial to cremation by a factor of about two to one. But whether it's having a solar-powered video screen embedded in your tombstone or arranging for your pallbearers to be dressed as Elvis Presley, traditional funerals are becoming more elaborate.

By 2025 Mr Dickinson expects more and more Americans will follow the lead of Hunter S Thompson. His 'cremains', at his request, last month were packed inside a firework and blasted from a cannon to a height of 500 feet above his home in Colorado.

Una McConville, a sociologist at Bath University whose special study is roadside memorials, argues that the rise in novel ways to commemorate death is not just a matter of egotism but reflects an ancient and deep-seated need to perform acts of public remembrance.

This is especially the case, she argues, with sudden and unexpected deaths, such as roadside accidents, or the 9/11 attacks on the World Trade Centre where there were few recoverable remains.

16 September 2005

Progress of cremation in the UK

Snapshot of the progress of cremation In the United Kingdom 1885-2004 (for full statistics, see www.srgw.demon.co.uk)

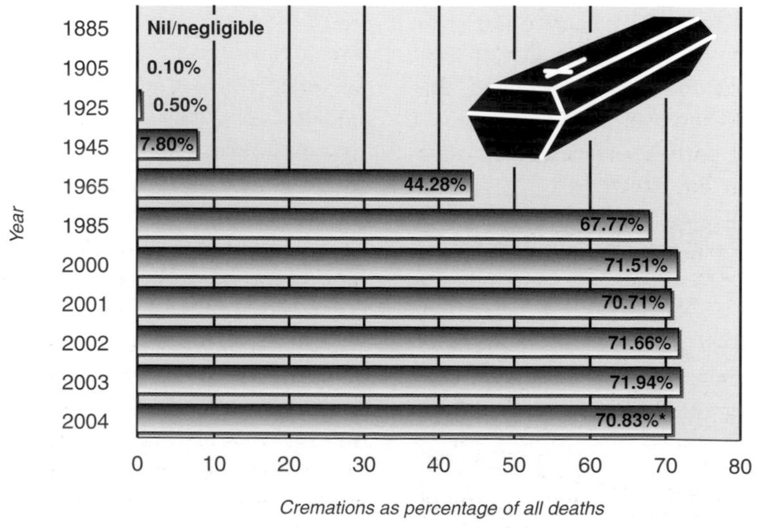

* Provisional figures as at 21st March 2005

Source: The Cremation Society of Great Britain

Types of burial

Information from If I Should Die

Traditional burial

Around thirty per cent of the population still choose to be buried in traditional churchyards and municipal cemeteries, which means that churches and municipal cemeteries have to find room for 160,000 new graves every year.

However, a critical shortage of space in existing churchyards is developing and most urban and suburban churchyards no longer have space available. In addition, some of Britain's major cities are already running out of cemetery space to bury the dead. It is reported that inner London boroughs have only seven years before they are completely full and even in outer London boroughs, there are only 18 years left.

The person who has died may already have arranged a grave space in a churchyard or cemetery which may be included in the will or papers. If space has already been paid for in a cemetery there will be a Deed of Grant, which should be amongst the deceased's papers.

Most cemeteries are non-denominational and are owned by local authorities or private companies and fees vary with plots costing anything from £30 to £5,000 depending on the location. People should be aware that because of pressure of space, particularly in bigger cities, most burial plots are now sold on a system of leasehold. Remains can therefore be moved to another part of the cemetery once the lease has expired.

Because the majority of cemeteries are non-denominational, most types of funeral service or ceremony can be conducted there. Advice will also be available from the ministers of the religion or religious organisation that the deceased may have belonged to.

If you want to be buried in a churchyard, you can find out from the priest or minister if space is available and the right to be buried there.

A burial will require the certificate for burial or cremation or if a coroner was involved, the order for burial.

Around thirty per cent of the population still choose to be buried in traditional churchyards and municipal cemeteries

The Registrar of Birth and Deaths will issue the Certificate for Burial or Cremation, which is a green certificate, or if a coroner was involved, the Order for Burial. This can be given to the funeral director or sent to the cemetery or crematorium.

As soon as the death has been certified, then plans for the funeral can go ahead and provisional bookings can be made at a cemetery, once the attendance of a minister (if required) has been arranged.

Forms required for burial

A Notice of Burial must be delivered to the cemetery authority as soon as a funeral booking is confirmed. This is a formal notification and forms a binding contract regarding the work and costs involved. The form should be accompanied by the Registrar's green certificate or the Coroner's Order for Burial.

A burial in Scotland requires the certificate of registration of death.

Cremation

Cremation used to be presented as the environmentally friendly option and with the pressure on the country's graveyards, it is still a popular choice, with about 70 per cent of the population choosing this option. However, there are increasing environmental concerns about the pollutants being released into the atmosphere.

EU laws governing emissions from crematoriums during the last ten years have led to most being updated and computerised. Since carbon particles are outlawed, crematoriums now emit only invisible gases. Contained within these are dangerous pollutants, including dioxins. Crematoriums are thought to be responsible for approximately 9% of airborne mercury emissions, caused by the combustion of dental amalgam, 12% of atmospheric dioxins, pollutants linked with cancer and other illnesses, and emissions of the chloride and formaldehyde used in the embalming process.

Most crematoriums are run by local authorities, although a number are operated by private companies. The costs usually include the medical referee's fee and the use of the chapel. Increasingly, due to obvious waste of burning a wooden coffin, more people are using cheaper coffins, often made of chipboard and even cardboard.

Most crematoriums allocate about 30-40 minutes for a service although some can be as short as 20 minutes.

It is important to make your wishes clear what you want done with the remains. Ashes can be scattered in a garden of remembrance or in a favourite spot (subject to the landowner's permission), buried in a churchyard or cemetery, or kept.

If no wishes have been expressed, it is the responsibility of the funeral director or crematorium staff to contact the relative before disposal. In the case of babies or very young children there may be no ashes following a cremation.

Arrangements can be made for the placing of a memorial plaque at some crematoriums, but there may be a charge for erecting one.

No one can be cremated until the cause of death is definitely known and a number of forms, available from the funeral director or crematorium, have to be completed. These are a form A and two doctors' certificates.

The Registrar of Births and Deaths will issue an Order for Burial or Cremation, which is a green certificate. This can be given to the funeral director or sent to the cemetery or crematorium.

More and more people are considering different sorts of funeral as an alternative to traditional religious services and cremations

As soon as the death has been certified, then plans for the funeral can go ahead and provisional bookings can be made at a crematorium, once the attendance of a minister (if required) has been arranged.

Forms required for cremation

No one can be cremated until the cause of death is definitely known and a number of forms, available from the funeral director or crematorium, have to be completed. These are a form A and two doctors' certificates.

- Form A – Application for Cremation – to be completed by the next of kin or an executor and needs countersigning by a householder who knows the person completing the form.
- Medical Forms B & C – statutory forms completed by the doctor who attended the deceased before death and the doctor who confirmed the cause of death (for which there will be a charge of about £82).
- Notice of Cremation – gives notice of the cremation and details of the deceased and information about the service. It forms a binding contract concerning the payment of fees to the cremation authority.

For cremation in Scotland, the certificate of registration of death, issued by the registrar, will need to be provided. In addition to the Application for Cremation and two cremation certificates signed by two doctors as above, a third crematorium certificate is required, signed by the medical referee at the crematorium.

Cremated remains

When choosing cremation, it is important to consider what to do with the remains. The crematorium will place the cremated remains in an inexpensive container which can be taken away. This will weigh in the region of 2kg (5-7lbs).

Many people scatter them in a spot of special significance to the deceased and the family. There is usually no restriction although in theory you should seek the permission of the landowner. My own father's ashes were scattered by my mother on his favourite trout fishing lake, where he spent many happy hours.

Others may choose to scatter or bury them in their own garden, but this option should be considered in the light of possibly moving house and whether you wish cremated remains to be eventually placed together, such as with a husband and wife.

Some people wish to place cremated remains in a cemetery or churchyard and you will need to check on the type of container that is acceptable to the location.

Crematoriums also have their own Gardens of Remembrance, which, although not consecrated, are dedicated to the dead of all religions and non-believers. Bereaved people can visit these gardens for some quiet solace and contemplation and memorials in the form of tree or shrub planting may be available. Placement of the remains by either spreading over the garden or burial in the garden is usually free of charge if the cremation took place there.

Memorials in the form of a Book of Remembrance or a memorial plaque may also be available.

Cremated remains can even be sent into space through a company in America called Celestis Services, see www.celestis.com.

Organising green/alternative/ DIY burials

More and more people are considering different sorts of funeral as an alternative to traditional religious services and cremations. Many of which are along more environmentally friendly lines such as woodland burials or burial at home if the size of the grounds allows it. In fact the choice continues to widen, with people sometimes sending their ashes into space.

One of the most popular alternatives to traditional burials and cremations are those in woodland or nature reserve burial grounds. It is also perfectly possible to arrange some aspects of the burial yourself, however it requires a degree of courage, planning and determination to undertake a complete DIY funeral.

A death certificate signed by a doctor and a certificate for burial from the registrar of deaths will be required if you are planning most of your own arrangements. However, if you are planning a private burial – which includes those not in a churchyard or cemetery – you must first register your intention of doing so. It is advisable to consult both the Environment Agency and the local council environmental health department about possible pollution of water courses.

Burial on private land

The burial of Princess Diana in the grounds at Althorp drew attention to the idea of being buried at home. Other household names such as Barbara Cartland and Jonny Morris have also chosen to be buried in the grounds of their own homes. However, if you are planning an interment of this type then a number of local authority permissions will need to be granted.

Even if you own the land concerned, you must check the deeds to ensure there are no restrictions on what the property may be used for. Although planning permission is not strictly necessary if you own the freehold, it is advisable to consult the local planning office and environmental health department who will want to ensure that the local water table will not be affected. It seems that if this is the desired choice, then you should talk to the appropriate authorities well in advance.

A burial at home is also likely to bring down the value of your home, possibly by up to 25 per cent. It is also worth bearing in mind the possible emotional and practical difficulties presented by moving house. Once remains have been buried, they may not be disturbed or removed without authority. Your family will have to face leaving the grave behind or else apply for a Home Office licence for exhumation.

A record of the burial should be made and kept with the deeds or other relevant documents relating to the land.

An alternative to burial is to scatter or bury the ashes from a cremation in the garden. Technically ashes that are buried are still subject to exhumation laws, but obviously it is much easier to move them if required.

'Green' funerals – woodland or nature reserve burial grounds

'Green burials' are becoming increasingly popular and there are a number of commercial sites opening around the country, promoting eco-friendly funerals and more informal ceremonies. These are often in woodland or nature reserve burial grounds of which there are currently about 50 already open in the UK, with at least another 50 applying for planning permission.

The Natural Death Centre has researched the laws and regulations for the UK surrounding burial on farmland and in large private gardens and recent cases have confirmed that no planning permission is required for 'a limited number of unmarked and unfenced graves'.

At woodland burial grounds relatives may be able to plant a tree to mark the site either on or near the grave. At nature reserve burial grounds, which can be wild flower meadows or pastures, graves are either unmarked or may be marked by a small wooden plaque that will rot away naturally and bulbs and flowers can be planted.

For those not using undertakers, cardboard and wooden coffins are obtainable, as well as woollen shrouds. However, an increasing number of undertakers will offer assistance with a woodland burial, such as providing transport of the body and cardboard coffins.

A list of woodland burial grounds is available from the Natural Death Centre.

The Natural Death Centre is an educational charity dedicated to supporting those dying at home and providing a movement to parallel the natural birth movement, including acting for the consumer It produces its own handbook, *The Natural Death Handbook* (13.50 inc p&p) which offers advice on all areas of organising a 'green burial' as well as aspects such as living wills. It also offers a good funeral guide, listing good funeral directors and good crematoria and cemeteries.

The Natural Death Centre
6 Blackstock Mews
Blackstock Road
London
N4 2BT
Tel: 020 7359 8391
Fax: 020 7354 3831
Email: rhino@dial.pipex.com
http://www.naturaldeath.org.uk/

DIY funerals

An increasing number of undertakers will offer advice (usually at an hourly rate) about organising a DIY funeral. Alternatively, see The New Natural Death Handbook for detailed information and advice on how to organise a completely DIY funeral.

Burial at sea

About 20 burials take place at sea each year. Apply to the Ministry of Agriculture for a licence which is free, but there are a large number of bureaucratic guidelines to discourage it. For a licence apply to the marine licensing person at the Ministry of Agriculture, Fisheries and Food (MAFF) on 020 238 5869 or contact your local Fisheries District Inspector.

If a sea burial is planned, you should tell the registrar when registering the death, so that a Coroner's Out of England Form (Form 104) and the local coroner's address to which it should be sent can be obtained from the registrar.

■ The above information is reprinted with kind permission from If I Should Die. If you would like to learn more, please visit their website at www.ifishoulddie.co.uk

KEY FACTS

■ People grieve in order to accept a deep loss and carry on with their life. Experts believe that if you do not grieve at the time of death, or shortly after, the grief may stay bottled up inside you. (page 1)

■ Some stages of grief are commonly experienced by people when they are bereaved. (page 1)

■ One in four adults will have experienced the death of someone close to them within the past five years. (page 3)

■ Bereavement counselling – long considered by psychologists to be vital in recovering from the death of a loved one – may be a waste of time, according to a new study. (page 6)

■ You may feel angry at the person who has died for leaving you on your own – you may feel guilty at having wished the person would die in cases for instance of a severely ill person who was suffering pain and a poor quality of life – these are perfectly normal feelings to have. (page 7)

■ It is common for anyone bereaved by suicide to blame themselves. (page 8)

■ Some bereavements are very hard to take in and make real. This is particularly likely if the loss is unexpected, we have been unable to see or hold the lost person or there is a delay in recovering or identifying them. (page 10)

■ As with any bereavement the death of a much loved pet can be devastating and an enormous loss. If you were close to your pet it is normal to have the reactions to its loss that you may experience in the death of a person. (page 13)

■ Many people feel that they shouldn't talk about the person that has died as this will bring on another wave of grief. However, most bereaved people say that they find it hurtful if the deceased is not mentioned, almost as if they had never existed. (page 15)

■ It is not uncommon to feel nothing at all after a bereavement. You may perhaps have a sense of disbelief and not be able or ready to believe that the person has died. (page 19)

■ Every 30 minutes, the mother or father of someone under 18 dies, which means that approximately two children and young people under 18 are bereaved of a parent every hour of every day in the UK. (page 20)

■ 3% of 5- to 15-year-olds have experienced the death of a parent or sibling; this equates to 255,000 young people in the UK. (page 20)

■ One of the most common assumptions made by people who haven't yet experienced the death of a relative or friend is that you must feel sad and weepy all of the time. You may, you may not. (page 21)

■ Children often feel guilty – that they somehow contributed directly or indirectly to the person's death. It is very common for a child to feel responsible for a family death. (page 27)

■ Research suggests that between 4 and 7 per cent of young people may lose a parent before age 16, and that a similar proportion experience the death of a sibling – most often the loss of a baby brother or sister. (page 28)

■ It is traditional to wear dark clothes to Christian funerals and black ties with suits, but sometimes, people prefer to wear bright clothes as a celebration of life and resurrection. (page 33)

■ Cremation is the traditional method of disposal of the body for members of the Sikh and Hindu religions. (page 34)

■ Both Muslims and Jews try to bury the body within 24 hours of death if possible. (page 34)

■ Humanists are non-religious people who live by moral principles based on reason and respect for others, not obedience to dogmatic rules. Humanist non-religious funeral ceremonies acknowledge loss and celebrate a life without employing religious rituals. (page 35)

■ In 2004, 70.83% of deceased people in the UK were cremated. (page 36)

■ A critical shortage of space in existing churchyards is developing and most urban and suburban churchyards no longer have space available. (page 37)

■ Crematoriums are thought to be responsible for approximately 9% of airborne mercury emissions, caused by the combustion of dental amalgam, 12% of atmospheric dioxins, pollutants linked with cancer and other illnesses, and emissions of the chloride and formaldehyde used in the embalming process. (page 37)

■ One of the most popular alternatives to traditional burials and cremations are those in woodland or nature reserve burial grounds. (page 38)

GLOSSARY

'Alternative' burial
A method of burying a dead body which deviates from the 'traditional' method of churchyard burial, for example burial in a woodland or nature reserve.

Bereavement
To experience a loss. This can be a loss of any kind, but the term is most commonly used to refer to losing someone through their death.

Cemetery
Also called a graveyard or churchyard. Area of land where graves are erected to the dead. It is usually found attached to a place of worship or a crematorium.

Cremation
A method of disposing of a dead body by burning. The ashes produced are given to the family of the deceased, who can either keep them (usually in an urn), or choose to scatter them – this is often in a favourite place of the deceased.

Crematorium
A building which carries out cremations.

Coffin
A box, usually wooden, in which the body is placed before burial or cremation.

Coroner
A doctor or lawyer responsbile for investigating deaths.

Eulogy
A speech delivered at a funeral, praising the person who has died and reminiscing about their life.

Executor
Someone responsbile for the administration of a person's estate after their death, usually nominated by the deceased in their will.

Funeral
The funeral is a ceremony, often faith-based and held in a church or other religious building, which friends and family of the deceased can attend as a way of saying goodbye to the dead person and remembering their life.

Grave
A hole dug in the ground in which a dead body is buried. It is usually marked by a gravestone.

Gravestone
Also known as a tombstone. A stone monument erected to a dead person, usually inscribed with their name, which friends and family can visit as a way of remembering the dead person. It is usually found in a cemetery.

Grief
An intense feeling of sorrow felt after a bereavement; the process of facing the loss of someone you love.

Mourner
Attendee at a funeral or other remembrance service for a deceased friend or relative.

Mourning
Also called grieving. A state in which an individual is in a state of grief. The phrase 'to be in mourning' is more specific – it suggests the observation of certain conventions, for example wearing black.

Obituary
Notice of a death, usually in a newspaper.

Post-mortem
A medical procedure carried out on a dead body to discover the cause of death if this is unclear.

Remembrance service
Also called a memorial service. Like a funeral, a remembrance service is a ceremony remembering someone's life, but it is held at a later time after someone has been buried or cremated. It may be a one-off ceremony, or it may occur on a regular basis, eg annually.

Traumatic bereavement
A traumatic bereavement is a loss which is unexpected, untimely, and often associated with horrific or frightening circumstances, such as death by suicide, murder or natural disaster.

Undertaker
Also known as the funeral director. A person who is responsible for organising funerals and preparing bodies for burial or cremation.

Widow
A woman whose husband has died.

Widower
A man whose wife has died.

Will
A legal document made by a person before their death, containing instructions about matters such as funeral arrangements and division of property in the event of their death.

INDEX

ADDITIONAL RESOURCES

Other* Issues *titles

If you are interested in researching further the issues raised in *Grief and Loss*, you may want to read the following titles in the ***Issues*** series as they contain additional relevant articles:

- Vol. 60 *Confronting Cancer* (ISBN 1 86168 230 1)
- Vol. 68 *Coping with Depression* (ISBN 1 86168 250 6)
- Vol. 72 *Obesity and Eating Disorders* (ISBN 1 86168 254 9)
- Vol. 75 *Lone-Parent Families* (ISBN 1 86168 264 6)
- Vol. 77 *Self-Inflicted Violence* (ISBN 1 86168 266 2)
- Vol. 84 *Mental Wellbeing* (ISBN 1 86168 279 4)
- Vol. 92 *Terrorism* (ISBN 1 86168 300 6)
- Vol. 93 *Binge Drinking* (ISBN 1 86168 301 4)
- Vol. 94 *Religions and Beliefs in Britain* (ISBN 1 86168 302 2)
- Vol. 100 *Stress and Anxiety* (ISBN 1 86168 314 6)
- Vol. 102 *The Ethics of Euthanasia* (ISBN 1 86168 316 2)
- Vol. 105 *Ageing Issues* (ISBN 1 86168 325 1)
- Vol. 114 *Drug Abuse* (ISBN 1 86168 347 2)
- Vol. 117 *Self-Esteem and Body Image* (ISBN 1 86168 350 2)

For more information about these titles, visit our website at www.independence.co.uk/publicationslist

Useful organisations

You may find the websites of the following organisations useful for further research:

- BUPA: www.bupa.co.uk
- The Child Bereavement Trust: www.childbereavement.org
- Civitas: www.civitas.org.uk
- The Cremation Society of Great Britain: www.srgw.demon.co.uk/CremSoc
- Cruse Bereavement Care: www.cruse.org.uk
- Handbag: www.handbag.com
- If I Should Die: www.ifishoulddie.co.uk
- The Joseph Rowntree Foundation: www.jrf.org.uk
- Marie Curie Cancer Care: www.mariecurie.org.uk
- Widowhood – a young woman's survival guide: www.merrywidow.me.uk
- Mind: www.mind.org.uk
- Pets2Rest: www.pets2rest.co.uk
- Pet Loss: www.petloss.com
- SupportLine: www.supportline.org.uk
- UK Funerals Online: www.uk-funerals.co.uk
- Winston's Wish: www.winstonswish.org.uk

ACKNOWLEDGEMENTS

The publisher is grateful for permission to reproduce the following material.

While every care has been taken to trace and acknowledge copyright, the publisher tenders its apology for any accidental infringement or where copyright has proved untraceable. The publisher would be pleased to come to a suitable arrangement in any such case with the rightful owner.

Chapter One: Bereavement Issues

Bereavement, © BUPA, *Understanding bereavement*, © Mind, *Grief counselling a waste of time, say psychologists*, © Telegraph Group Limited 2006, *Feelings on bereavement*, © SupportLine, *Traumatic bereavements*, © Cruse, *When a parent dies*, © handbag.com, *Pet bereavement*, © SupportLine, *Helping the bereaved*, © If I Should Die, *Remembering*, © The Child Bereavement Trust, *Mourning sickness feeds the feel-good factor*, © Guardian Newspapers Limited 2006.

Chapter Two: Grief and Young People

Teenage grief, © Marie Curie Cancer Care, *Bereavement – frequently asked questions*, © Winston's Wish, *Myths about grief*, © Winston's Wish, *What's OK and what's not*, © The Child Bereavement Trust, *Questions about death*, © Marie Curie Cancer Care, *Better help urged for bereaved young people*, © Joseph Rowntree Foundation.

Chapter Three: Handling the Formalities

A checklist, © Crown copyright is reproduced with permission from Her Majesty's Stationery Office, *When someone dies*, © Cruse Bereavement care, *After a death*, © UK Funerals Online, *Religious traditions*, © If I Should Die, *Alternative burials*, © Guardian Newspapers Limited 2005, *Types of burial*, © If I Should Die.

Photographs and illustrations:

Pages 1, 27, 35: Angelo Madrid; pages 6, 18, 29: Simon Kneebone; pages 7, 24, 33: Don Hatcher; pages 10, 39: Pumpkin House; page 38: Bev Aisbett.

Craig Donnellan
Cambridge
April, 2006